IN THE HA

IN THE HALL OF MIRRORS

Some Problems of Commitment
in a Religiously Plural World

The Gifford Research Fellowship Lectures for 1985,
delivered at St Mary's College, University of St Andrews

C. J. Arthur

MOWBRAY
LONDON & OXFORD

Copyright © C. J. Arthur 1986

ISBN 0 264 67090 6

First published 1986
by A. R. Mowbray & Co. Ltd,
Saint Thomas House, Becket Street,
Oxford, OX1 1SJ

Typeset by Acorn Bookwork, Salisbury, Wiltshire
Printed in Great Britain by Biddles Ltd, Guildford

British Library Cataloguing in Publication Data

Arthur, C. J.
  In the hall of mirrors: some problems
  of commitment in a religiously plural world.
  —(The Gifford Research Fellowship
  lectures for 1985)
  1. Religions
  I. Title II. Series
  291   BL80.2

  ISBN 0-264-67090-6

Everyone has the right to freedom of thought, conscience and religion; this right includes freedom to change his religion or belief, and freedom, either alone or in a community with others and in public or private, to manifest his religion or belief in teaching, practice, worship and observance.

Article 18, The United Nations Universal
Declaration of Human Rights

THIS BOOK IS DEDICATED TO THOSE WHO
ARE DENIED CIPHER'S FREEDOM TO
CHOOSE WHAT TO BELIEVE IN

The author's royalties from the sale of this volume have been donated to Amnesty International

Contents

Preface

This book consists of the slightly revised text of the Gifford Research Fellowship Lectures which I delivered at St Mary's College, University of St Andrews, in the Spring of 1985.

The terms of Lord Gifford's Bequest to the older universities of Scotland have become well known through the Gifford Lectures which, for nearly a hundred years now, have provided a unique forum for scholarship in the general area of natural theology.

Although designed to encourage the work of those at a more junior level than that customarily occupied by the Gifford Lecturers, the Gifford Research Fellowship is also governed by the terms which Lord Gifford laid down in 1885. In particular, the fellow is required, during his year's appointment, to give a series of public lectures which will be accessible to the interested lay person, rather than being geared solely for a specialist audience.

It is no doubt inviting criticism of shallowness, to try to traverse in so few pages such an extensive and difficult area as that represented by the hall of mirrors. I am mindful that, at almost every point along the way, a critic would only have to exert the least interrogatory pressure to leave the discussion bogged down in a mire of unresolved problems. That the ground has been covered so quickly, with so many topographical complexities simply ignored or hurriedly skated over, has to do with the awareness that there are more appropriate places to engage in that intellectual mud-wrestling so beloved by academics than a series of lectures governed by the terms of the Gifford Bequest.

It is daunting and inspiring to stand at the beginning of what may become a (minor) tradition. I can only hope that in these days of belt tightening in higher education, the Gifford

Committee at St Andrews will try to ensure continuity so that these lectures will not have the dubious distinction of being both first and last to be given under the auspices of the Gifford Research Fellowship.

I am particularly grateful to Professor William McKane, Principal of St Mary's College, Professor D. W. D. Shaw, Dean of the Faculty of Divinity, Professor J. A. Whyte, Mr J. M. Keeling, Dr G. B. Hall, Dr J. S. Alexander and Dr A. J. M. Wedderburn for kindly agreeing to chair the lectures, and to Mr Clarke Geddes, Director of Adult Education and Extra Mural Studies, for organizing programmes and publicity.

Finally, it seems apt to remember Lord Gifford himself, that earnest inquirer after truth, without whose generosity Cipher and all his works might never have been conceived.

St Mary's College   CHRIS ARTHUR
St Andrews
December 1985

Acknowledgements

For permission to reproduce material from works under copyright, grateful acknowledgement and thanks are extended to the following individuals and organizations:

The Society for Promoting Christian Knowledge for extracts from *The Meaning and End of Religion* (1978) by Wilfred Cantwell Smith.

Collins Publishers for an extract from *Beyond Ideology, Religion and the Future of Western Civilization* (1981) by Ninian Smart.

Oxford University Press for extracts from *The Sense of God* (1973) and *The Religious Imagination and the Sense of God* (1978) by John Bowker, *Speculum Mentis* (1924) by R. G. Collingwood, *Beyond Existentialism and Zen* (1979) by George Rupp, *Mankind and Mother Earth* (1976) by Arnold Toynbee, and *The Idea of the Holy* (1977) by Rudolf Otto, translated by John W. Harvey.

University of California Press for extracts from *The Sword and the Flute, Kali and Krishna, Dark Visions of the Terrible and the Sublime in Hindu Mythology* (1975) by David R. Kinsley.

Random House, Inc. for an extract from *The Autobiography of Benvenuto Cellini*, translated by John Addington Symonds.

Mrs Laura Huxley and Chatto & Windus Ltd for extracts from *Those Barren Leaves* (1925) and *The Perennial Philosophy* (1946) by Aldous Huxley.

Falmer Press Ltd for an extract from Lesslie Newbigin's 'Teaching Religion in a Secular Plural Society' from *New*

Directions in Religious Education (1982), ed. by John Hull.

The Revd Master Daishin Morgan for an extract from 'Choosing your Way' in the Journal of Throssel Hole Priory Vol. X, No. I.

Penguin Books Ltd for extracts from *Exploring Inner Space* (1982) by David Hay, copyright © David Hay, 1982.

Muller, Blond & White Ltd for an extract from *The Soul of the White Ant* (1937) by Eugene Marais.

University of Notre Dame Press for an extract from *The Forbidden Forest* by Mircea Eliade, © 1978 by University of Notre Dame Press.

The Aristotelian Society for an extract from 'Gods' by John Wisdom, in the *Proceedings of the Aristotelian Society for 1944–45*, © The Aristotelian Society, 1944. Reprinted by courtesy of the Editor.

Faber and Faber Ltd (Publishers) for extracts from *Death of an Expert Witness* (1977) by P. D. James and *The Ten Principal Upanishads* (1970) translated by Shree Purohit Swami and W. B. Yeats.

SCM Press Ltd for an extract from *A Dialogue of Religions* (1960) by Ninian Smart.

Mouton de Gruyter for extracts from *Principles of Integral Science of Religion* (1979) by Georg Schmid.

Macmillan Publishing Co. for an extract from *The Secret of Father Brown* (1927) by G. K. Chesterton. Reprinted with permission of Macmillan Publishing Company, originally published by Cassell & Co. Ltd.

Routledge & Kegan Paul for an extract from *The Agony of Christianity and Essays on Faith* (1974) by Miguel de Unamuno, translated by Anthony Kerrigan.

Grafton Books, a division of the Collins Publishing Group, for an extract from *At Swim Two Birds* (1939) by Flann O'Brien.

Simon & Schuster Inc. for an extract from *Religion in the Secular City* (1984) by Harvey Cox.

Frederick Streng for an extract from his book *Emptiness: A Study in Religious Meaning* (1967).

Harper & Row, New York, for extracts from *Introduction to Religion, a Phenomenological Approach* (1968) by Winston L. King and *The Purposes of Higher Education* (1955) by Huston Smith.

Wilfred Cantwell Smith for extracts from *Questions of Religious Truth* (1967).

1

Introducing Cipher and the Hall of Mirrors

In the early pages of that oddest of books, Flann O'Brien's *At Swim Two Birds*, we read how the proprietor of the Red Swan Hotel, Mr Dermot Trellis, gives birth to a fully grown man. An extract from the local press reports that

the new arrival, stated to be 'doing very nicely', is about 5 feet 8 inches in height, well-built, dark and clean shaven.[1]

Trellis is, of course, a writer and the new arrival – one John Furriskey by name – is the intended villain in his book. However, the author's plans go seriously awry when he becomes so involved in his own fictional world that he seduces the leading lady, and is eventually put on trial for his life by a self-appointed court of rebellious characters who are ill-pleased with the lot assigned to them by their creator. At that trial Trellis is cross-examined about the nature of Furriskey's birth:

'In what manner was he born?,' the court asks.
'He awoke,' replies Trellis, 'as if from sleep.'
'What were his sensations?'
'Bewilderment, perplexity. He was consumed by doubts as to his own identity.'[2]

In an effort to dispel these doubts, Furriskey is seen, shortly after his impromptu entrance into the world,

searching his room for a looking glass or for a surface that would enable him to ascertain the character of his countenance.[3]

The court is particularly enraged at Trellis' seeming indifference to the severe mental anguish he has occasioned by

1

creating a character who is left so uncertain about who he is and what he ought to do.

'Why,' they ask him, 'did you not perform so obvious an errand of mercy as to explain his identity and duties to him?'[4]

To this, Trellis has no answer.

Miles away from Flann O'Brien's riotous imagination, in David Hume's *Enquiry Concerning Human Understanding*, we find a not entirely dissimilar process of birth when Hume introduces the man brought into the world 'on a sudden',[5] fully adult and with all his sensory faculties functioning correctly, yet with absolutely no prior experience of the empirical world. Hume's creation is brought on to support the argument against necessary connection. He is given no name, allowed no benefit from custom, 'the great guide of human life',[6] and once he has served his role as dumb (and, we must presume, utterly disorientated) advocate of Hume's philosophical point of view, he disappears without trace. Unlike the unfortunate Trellis, Hume – so far as we know – was never brought to book for so capricious an act of creation.

It is from a birth not unlike that of John Furriskey or of Hume's man brought into the world on a sudden, that I wish to begin this exploration of commitment in a religiously plural world. The character I wish to bring to life – and whose fortunes I will follow in the seven chapters of this book – will be similar to Furriskey in that he will feel bewilderment, perplexity and immense doubt about his identity and purpose, and, like Furriskey, he will search for a mirror which may reveal the 'true character of his (and the world's) counte-nance'; he is similar to Hume's abruptly born man in that he has been deliberately created to serve a particular purpose – though, as will become instantly apparent, none of my argu-ments display a Humean elegance or concision.

I shall call my creature *Cipher*. The name is chosen simply because so many of its resonances of meaning are appropriate to his situation. To begin with, Cipher in the sense of nought or zero suggests *neutrality*, something bearing neither plus or minus value. Secondly, although this neutral zero may have no value in itself, it is something which, placed behind any integer, any whole number, multiplies its value tenfold. Thirdly, Cipher can be suggestive of code, of some secret mode of writing where the meaning is uncertain until we find the key which acts to de-cipher what is said. Fourthly, Cipher suggests a person of little significance, a non-entity, someone whose existence and individuality tend to be dwarfed by the immensity or multiplicity of the environing phenomena. All these senses are quite deliberately implicit in the name which I have chosen, and I will explain their aptness in due course.[7]

Who, then, is Cipher and in what situation does he find himself? Adopting Martin Hollis' neat formula for 'in a nutshell' replies,[8] a miser summarizing an answer to these questions by telegram could do so in ten words: *Cipher is someone perplexed by a situation of religious plurality*. In this chapter I want to go beyond such a miser's reply and concentrate on making clear the nature of his perplexity. We can then go on to consider how it might be resolved.

Cipher is an individual whose life is regularly punctuated by an unnerving sense of apparent insignificance, mystery and meaninglessness. His life appears insignificant when it is viewed against the back-drop of space, time, other persons' lives and the apparent accidentalness of fate. For Cipher knows something of the smallness of our planet and the scale on which individual existence upon it may be seen. In his informed mind's eye he sees the earth as an infinitesimal spark of light in a surrounding immensity of darkness. He knows that on its surface millions upon millions of human beings have passed the briefness of their hurried finitude, leaving scattered behind a cumulative history which dwarfs any single contributory existence such as his, in the same way that human history itself is dwarfed by the millions of years before its advent when the globe was untroubled by any human movement but bore only the unreflective tread of giant reptiles and amphibians upon its already ancient contours. He realizes that during his brief existence his life may go through pendulum swings of fortune so vast and inexplicable as to disturb any comforting equilibrium which a more reliable routine might suggest. To borrow a potent example recounted by George Steiner, one moment may see him as a comfortably housed academic gently pursuing the life of knowledge, the next as a tortured inmate of some dark place like Treblinka.[9] Less dramatically, one moment he may be in the peak of health and well-being and the next struck down by some accident, whether of natural or human origin, to some pitiful state of pain and incapacity.

At the same time as it may appear insignificant, Cipher's life also seems mysterious − indeed the very sense of its insignificance may act *to trigger* a sense of wonder and mystery. For is it not profoundly strange that amidst the ponderous immensities of time, space and circumstance, this one unique and fragile path which is his life should have emerged out of all the flux of seeming accidentalness and other possibilities? Why *this* path and not some other? That he should have been born at all and that being born he was born *thus*, as a particular individual, seems so improbable that the mere fact of his existence is replete with mystery.

Cipher has a wealth of knowledge at his disposal concerning the physical nature of the world he lives in and about the structure and function of the organism which he thinks of as 'me'. Around him science produces sophistication upon sophistication which can subdue and control much that hitherto was beyond all but the most minimal human influence, and, in terms of both sciences and humanities, his understanding of many aspects of his experience is subtle and profound. But yet there remains a sense of mystery which seems impervious to all the information he can muster, to all the power − practical and intellectual − which is at his disposal, and which seems even to mock the most accomplished technological achievements as being somehow beside the point. Why does he exist at all? And, existing, why in this particular form? Why is there something rather than nothing, why is there existence rather than unbroken emptiness? And, more pressingly, what view ought he to take of this mysterious place in which he briefly finds himself, such that his life may be lived in the most appropriate fashion?

Finally, Cipher's insignificant and mysterious life often

seems *meaningless*. Although he has many plans and ambitions, much that he wishes to do and much he would prefer to avoid, Cipher feels an underlying emptiness which does not allow such things to provide a fully satisfactory sense for his existence. Beneath his search for a better job, for increased wealth, for a happy family life, Cipher feels a deep absence of purpose. This sense of meaninglessness, like that of insignificance and mystery, is sharply accentuated by his encounter with the fact of suffering. He is aware that, although his own situation may be presently benign, peaceful and enjoyable, this is a precarious state. Moreover, there are always others in the grip of some variety of pain and horror. And of course, no matter how pleasant an existence may be, it will eventually be aborted. Death casts a shadow of futility even into Cipher's summer.

I will refer to Cipher's feelings of insignificance, mystery and meaninglessness collectively – since there is considerable overlap between them, both in terms of cause and expression – simply as his sense of *lostness*, a feeling that he does not belong in the world, that he possesses no sense of a place in it. Virginia Woolf once remarked that

the strange thing about life is that though the nature of it must have been apparent to everyone for hundreds of years, no one has left an adequate account of it.[10]

Cipher shares this sense of perplexity. No matter how at home he may often feel in the world, no matter how well acquainted with the familiar calms and turbulences of the human condition, he is periodically aware of his lack of any adequate account of life, of some statement about it, some outlook on it, some means of living it, which would quieten his feelings of insignificance, mystery and meaninglessness and comfort his lostness with an unshakeable sense of homecoming.

Alongside his sense of lostness, Cipher is well aware that there exist many versions of the 'adequate account of life' which he seeks. He recognizes that, since the dawn of history, people have found a sense of belonging in some form of religious outlook on life. From the burial ceremonies of early

man to the complexities of Vedic ritual, from the sacrifices –
sometimes human – which the Iron Age peoples of Europe
made to Nerthus, their earth goddess, to the Buddhists'
Eightfold Path, from the teachings of Jesus to Islamic submission to the will of Allah, Cipher sees glimpses of various
'adequate accounts' which seem to make sense of human
existence and seem to provide those who hold (or held) to
them with an effective defence against that intrusive sense of
lostness which troubles him.

Cipher sees many threads of purported sense which have
variously led men through the labyrinth of existence, plotting
guidelines across even such desolate places as those occupied
by pain and loneliness, separation and death. The problem is,
which, if any, should *he* follow? Do any of the religions offer
an adequate account of life which he can accept as such and, if
so, which one? Moreover, if such an account is to be found in
the religious realm, which one – or which combination –
offers the *most* adequate account? Cipher's situation is problematic, not simply because of a sense of lostness, but because
this is coupled with an awareness of numerous versions of
curative meaning which *might* counteract it. At this stage
anyway, his problem is not so much that of a man suffering
from some ailment who is looking for a cure, as that of
someone faced with trying to decide among many possible
treatments. He does not know which one is best or if a
combination would, perhaps, be better. Nor is he sure if they
offer the same diagnosis, or if *any* of them are, in fact,
efficacious.

To a large extent, Cipher's world is that of an educated
twentieth century Westerner. Now this is *not* to say either
that every contemporary educated Westerner may be characterized thus, or that in other times and places there was no
such thing as religious pluralism or that one must be educated
before being stung with a sense of life's insignificance, its
meaninglessness or mystery. However, our present century
and culture do have certain features which render Cipher's
situation problematic in a more insistent way than it might
have been, had I decided to bring him to birth in some other
setting. The first century Mediterranean would doubtless have

provided him with an interesting pluralism of beliefs, as the Christian religion budded towards its eventual global dimension in modest local settings of considerable spiritual diversity; whereas a genesis some centuries earlier in the midst of the plague in Athens, described so eloquently by Thucydides,[11] or in the turbulence of revolutionary France or Russia, might well be supposed potent enough environments to stir even the most complacent and untroubled outlook to thoughts of the insignificance and apparent senselessness of human life. Such settings would provide many interesting problems, but they are not ones I wish to investigate here. *Cipher is very much a twentieth century creation, located firmly in the present.*

Cipher's present-day status means that, rather than seeing no further than the next village or city or continent, his perspective is global. He is aware of the earth as a single planet and of its tinyness in space. And through the various cognitive telescopes and microscopes afforded by modern learning he can see, almost at a glance, the diversity of the present, and, stretching out before it, he can eavesdrop far beyond those ancestors whose lives and beliefs are still held warm in living memories, to generations long forgotten by any self-conscious familial survivor. Ninian Smart has drawn attention to the change in religious awareness from local to global dimensions which has been witnessed in the last century. Whereas in times past a religious consciousness could develop in relative isolation, in ignorance of what Smart calls 'other worlds' which exist beyond the horizon of its awareness, the present outlook can take virtually the whole gamut of human religiousness into its purview. Previously it was possible to be aware of religious diversity on a local scale, presently such awareness is of potentially global extent. As Smart writes in *Beyond Ideology*, his study of religion and the future of western civilization,

when Jesus walked with his comrades beside the hot blue shore of the lake, the Buddha's message was [unbeknownst to them] already centuries old in the minds of the shaven-headed monks of Sri Lanka. And men who went for a change of soul to the shining mysteries of Isis knew nothing of Confucius or the Tao. But now there is no world beyond our world. Our *oikumene* is spherical, closed, and there is no new frontier.[12]

Until the arrival of those extra-terrestrial beings whose existence some are so sure of, our outlook on religion may be considered complete, in a sense that was not possible for previous ages. In this global village, Cipher is aware of more religions than would have been possible at any other time – not because there *are* more, but because of the overview which is now available to him.

In the general context of 'modernity', Peter Berger has drawn attention to the 'multiplication of options'[13] facing man today. Indeed he suggests that 'modern consciousness entails a movement from fate to choice'.[14] Cipher is situated very much in the context of choice amidst multiple options. Fate has not dictated what account of the world he will accept as adequate; rather it has informed him of a range of possibilities and the decision is left to him. George Rupp has pointed out the way in which such a state of perceived pluralism poses a challenge, as it impinges ever more forcefully on the mind. In his *Beyond Existentialism and Zen* he argues that:

Greater self-consciousness about pluralism has the effect of radicalizing its impact. Unreflective awareness that other people adhere to different traditions becomes instead a recognition of multiple perspectives as alternatives competing for the individual's allegiance.[15]

Moreover, for Cipher the impact of pluralism is further radicalized by the fact that he approaches it from a perspective which is 'unanchored'. He is not a Christian or a Jew or a Hindu or a Muslim surveying the teachings of faiths other than his own – or, indeed, the variety of outlooks *within* his own faith – and coming to *theological* terms with the diversity; rather he is aware of the different religions' 'adequate accounts' of the world from a neutral, uncommitted perspective. He has no *religious* guidelines to which to appeal.

Let it be emphasized that, although he is definitely contemporary, I am not casting Cipher in any widely representative, let alone prescriptive, role. He does not stand for the plight of twentieth century religiousness, if indeed there is one; he is not meant to show how we *ought* to react to a situation of religious pluralism, even supposing such a single right way exists; his dilemma is not that of modern man in search of a soul, if that is indeed what modern man is looking for; he has not been designed to symbolize any problems which faith may encounter in a secular setting. I would hope that the situation in which I place him is not implausible, to the point of finding no resonance of interest or sympathy from his readers; but, at the same time, it must be stressed that his situation *is* to some extent artificial and contrived. Thus, if I had cared to make him modern in the sense of representing one widespread modern attitude towards religion, I ought, if Hendrik Kraemer's analysis is accurate, to have ensured that Cipher manifested that 'mysterious phenomenon' of complete indifference to religion — indifference in the face of extensive information — rather than the interest and concern which he will, in fact, show.[16] I would expect many people to see Cipher's whole character as improbable, and his search for some curative response to his sense of lostness to be fundamentally misguided. Indeed, I shall consider some powerful objections to it in a moment. It is, however, my intention to focus closely on this particular situation — for it seems preferable to discuss a single clearly demarcated example and let others draw their own conclusions about the extent of its relevance, rather than to make pronouncements on such elusive entities as 'modern religiousness', 'twentieth century spirituality' or whatever. Although it might seem unduly restrictive to focus in so closely on a particular figure, and an imaginary one at that, I would argue that, in so doing, quite apart from side-stepping the considerable perils of addressing highly contentious generalities, we may make appeal to various persuasive literary precedents as justifying such a strategy. For surely a great deal may be learned by looking closely at carefully constructed fictional settings — even if they are not, indeed perhaps *especially* if they are not, wholly typical of a particular age or group. Although Cipher can lay no claim to the status of a Hamlet, a Raskolnikov, an Anna Karenina or a Kristin Lavransdatter – beside them he is a mere shadow of ideas – he can claim credibility by appeal to the educative aspect of such fictions, which is unimpaired even when their situation is non-representative and their behaviour eccentric or indeed mad. It would, in short, be rather rash to question the usefulness of taking Cipher as a point of focus simply on the grounds of his individual fictional status.

From birth, albeit of the artificial ready-made kind which Flann O'Brien dubs 'aestho-autogamy',[17] let us go momentarily to death. In one of P. D. James' rather superior 'whodunnits', *Death of an Expert Witness*, we find Commander Adam Dalgleish and Detective Inspector Massingham searching through the room of a murder victim. Among his books are volumes by Teilhard de Chardin, Jean Paul Sartre and Plato, as well as numerous volumes on comparative religion. Massingham remarks to his chief:

'It looks as if he was one of those men who torment themselves trying to discover the meaning of existence.'
'You find that reprehensible?' Dalgleish asks.
'I find it futile. Metaphysical speculation is about as pointless as a discussion on the meaning of one's lungs, they're for breathing.'
'And life is for living. You find that an adequate personal credo?'
'To maximize one's pleasures and minimize one's pain, yes Sir, I do. And, I suppose, to bear with stoicism those miseries I can't avoid.'[18]

If Cipher were to meet an untimely end under suspicious circumstances and attract the attentions of such philosophical policemen, they would doubtless find in his room a similar preponderance of books on comparative religion, and it is clear that he would fall squarely into the category of 'one of those men who torment themselves trying to discover the meaning of existence'. Equally clear is the fact that there are many who would simply dismiss such an effort as futile and misconceived. How would Cipher reply to them?

He may well end up *agreeing* with them. Perhaps, in the end, his zero of neutrality will take its stand behind whatever integer indicates the value thus given to a life, by a decision which concludes that there is no meaning to existence beyond day to day criteria of sense, and that to look beyond these for some sort of *ultimate* purpose is simply misguided. It must be stressed that as we join him Cipher is uncommitted. His problem is not just to decide which religious outlook is true, for among the multiplicity of options apparently available to him is that which queries the reliability of *any* religious outlook. He does not begin by assuming *a priori* that some religious outlook on the world is true and that he only has to decide which one (which, obviously, would not be an easy task). Rather, his question is: which, *if any*, of these outlooks can offer an adequate account of life? Cipher's main assumption is that for many of their millions of believers, religious outlooks on the world provide precisely that antidote to a sense of lostness which he is looking for. Whether or not he will reach a similar conclusion about any of them remains uncertain.

For convenience I will refer to that state of mind in which no decision has been taken about the overall meaning and nature of existence, or about whether such a meaning exists, as '*world uncertainty*', to the resolution of this sense – in whatever form – as the discovery of '*world certainty*', and to the movement between former and latter states as making a '*world decision*'. Not all world certainties are religious, but I will be restricting my attention here to those of them which are. Thus, it is important to remember that making a world decision may as easily involve a rejection of any form of religious outlook as the acceptance of one.

Further, when we identify Cipher with the man who torments himself looking for the meaning of existence, we must avoid thinking in simplistic terms of his expecting a neat clearly formulated answer – such as the proverbial '42' in *The Hitch Hiker's Guide to the Galaxy*.[19] As Karl Britton puts it in his study of *Philosophy and the Meaning of Life*, 'To say that there is a meaning in life is to say that there is something that may serve as a guide in our lives.'[20] Cipher is not looking for some sort of verbal formula, but rather for some guidelines by which he can navigate a sense-giving course through the various elements of that feeling of lostness which prompts his sense of world uncertainty and which, together with his multi-religious informedness, lies at the root of his dilemma.

Rather than presenting Cipher as looking for 'the meaning of life' – which in the current *zeitgeist*, given such phenomena as Zaphod Beeblebrox and Monty Python, has become a topic in the preserve of the clown rather than the contemplative, we might simply say that Cipher is looking for *peace of mind* – which, according to the present Dalai Lama is, in the last analysis, 'the hope of all men.'[21] If such peace of mind does indeed exist, however, it ought to be stressed that most of the varieties of it offered in religious contexts do not exactly conform to an over-literal understanding of this phrase. Like that exemplar of educatively misleading titles, *Zen and the Art of Motorcycle Maintenance*,[22] a book which has little to do either with Zen or with motorcycle maintenance, 'peace of mind' may seem neither particularly peaceful nor primarily intellectual.

In terms of his religious environment, Cipher finds himself located in a *hall of mirrors*. Rather than standing before any single mirror – whether of Christianity, Hinduism, tribal animism or whatever – Cipher finds himself *surrounded* by mirrors, on which appear many differing reflections, purporting to show how he should see himself and the world he lives in and, in consequence, how he ought to conduct his life. The hall of mirrors is the first of many metaphors which I shall employ in exploring Cipher's situation. Indeed, as a general epigraph applicable to the book as a whole, I might have chosen Max Black's remark on the unique usefulness of metaphor:

Metaphorical thought is a distinctive mode of achieving insight, not to be construed as an ornamental substitute for plain thought.[23]

Since the hall of mirrors is the central metaphor to which I will refer, it is important to see how it can be used to symbolize many of the important aspects of the milieu in which Cipher is located. There are six points about it which I want to consider now.

Firstly, as we have already noted briefly, the hall of mirrors has always been there — though its extent and content will vary somewhat from age to age. It is *not* a twentieth century construction. Being in a position to *see* its existence is, however, a relatively recent phenomenon. Like the sky, religious pluralism has always, at least to some extent, been a characteristic of the human environment. But just as the jet aircraft is a comparatively recent innovation, so too is the ability to travel through the hall of mirrors to the extent and with the ease that it is now possible for us to do. That is not to say that previous generations never got airborne — but their passage through the religious hall of mirrors was of limited duration and questionable value, so imperfectly did they perceive the images which were there. Even so skilled a pioneer aviator in the inter-religious stratosphere as William Beveridge can be seen crashing through a low altitude survey of Judaism, Hinduism and Islam to land back where he had started from, almost as if he had never taken off. This is in no way to denigrate his efforts. That a passage from his *Private Thoughts Concerning Religion*, published posthumously in 1709, was chosen to preface that epoch-making entry into the hall of mirrors, *The Sacred Books of the East* series, is testimony to the enduring applicability of his *intentions* — even if the right equipment simply did not exist which would have allowed him to carry them out properly. Beveridge writes:

The general inclinations which are naturally implanted in my soul to some religion, it is impossible for me to shift off; but there being such a multiplicity ⟨ religions in the world, I desire now seriously to consider with myself, which of them all to restrain these my general inclinations to.[24]

Similar sentiments might be voiced by Cipher. The main differences between him and Beveridge would be: firstly, that whilst Beveridge moves out from — indeed never really leaves — a solid Christian base, Cipher has no such secure spiritual anchorage; secondly, whilst Beveridge considers it impossible that he should ever shake off the 'general inclinations' to some

religion that are 'implanted in his soul', Cipher's inclinations
to some religious outlook on the world are strongly connected
with his desire for peace of mind. If he finds that no such
peace of mind is available, *his* inclinations will be to dismiss
religion and look elsewhere; finally – and perhaps the greatest
difference between them – the meagreness of information
available to Beveridge simplifies his quest considerably, whilst
the range and depth of Cipher's information makes his search
a much more complex affair. Beveridge writes,

> the reason of this my inquiry is not that I am, in the least, dissatisfied
> with that religion I have already embraced; but because it is natural
> for all men to have an over-bearing opinion and esteem of that
> particular religion they are born and bred up in . . . to profess myself
> a Christian, and to believe that Christians are only in the right
> because my forefathers were so, is no more than the heathens and
> Mahometans have to say for themselves. Indeed, there was never any
> religion so barbarous and diabolical, but it was preferred before all
> other religions whatsoever, by them that did profess it. . . . The
> Indians that worship the devil, would think it as strange doctrine to
> say that Christ is to be feared more than the devil as such as believe in
> Christ think it to say the devil is to be preferred before Christ.[25]

For Cipher, the reason for his inquiry is similar to Beveridge's
in that birth alone does not serve to decide the matter of his
religion. He has not been born Hindu, Christian, Buddhist or
whatever, and thought no more about it. Unlike Beveridge,
though, whose realization of the inadequacy of mere indigen-
ousness as a justification for his faith does not, at the same
time, mean that he abandons his world-certain position for
one of neutral investigator – in anything more than an artificial methodological sense – for Cipher there is no such point
of reference to set off from or return to. Moreover, whilst
Beveridge can dismiss the 'heathens' and 'Mahometans' fairly
easily as worshipping devils or being otherwise grossly misled,
Cipher has abandoned such an instantly dismissive vocabulary, with all its easy theological implications, as he discovers
more and more about the religions in question and recognizes
their status as serious attempts to offer an 'adequate account
of the world'. The hall of mirrors is not new, but never before

have so many of its polished surfaces been accessible to the inquiring eye.

The second feature of the hall of mirrors which I want to stress is that it may have either a theoretical or concrete locus – or a mixture of both. In other words, Cipher might be informed about Hinduism, Buddhism, Christianity, Islam etc. in a theoretical fashion only, without having actually encountered any living representatives of these faiths, or he might have no knowledge about the different religions beyond what can be observed in the people around him. Since this is not a sociological inquiry, I will assume that for Cipher the hall of mirrors is perceived more as a theoretical than an actual structure, that his main information about it comes from reading and thinking widely in the general area of religious studies and comparative religion, rather than from encountering it in day to day life. However, given his status as a contemporary, as a firmly twentieth century creature, it seems only appropriate to assume that Cipher's theoretical knowledge about the hall of mirrors will be supplemented by those more concrete, practical inputs afforded by living in an increasingly multi-cultural and therefore multi-religious society.

Thirdly, the religious hall of mirrors must not be seen in the simplistic terms suggested by the fairground version of this phenomenon, from which the metaphor is, admittedly, derived. It is not as if we enter some dim-lit tent and walk between a row of mirrors showing four deviations from the norm: fat, thin, squat and tall, knowing all along what we really look like, and feeling amusement rather than puzzlement. Cipher has not *chosen* to enter the hall of mirrors, and he can see no easy exit from it which marks a return to normality. He does not know all along what the correct image is, nor are there a mere handful of reflections before him. It is not as if he is flanked on one side by Hinduism, Buddhism and Taoism and on the other by Judaism, Christianity and Islam, such that there are six distinct images, six adequate accounts of the world, offering the possibility of peace of mind in the face of his feelings of insignificance, mystery and meaninglessness.

Apart from the fact that inter-religious diversity extends
beyond those faiths just mentioned to Jainism, Shinto, Sikhism, Zoroastrianism, and into the uncertain area of modern
religious movements and what Tillich termed the quasi-
religions (such things as Marxism), there is considerable
intra-religious diversity as well. Each mirror which we might
at first sight take to be single is, in fact, fragmented into many
facets. The various religions do not simply present a series of
single unitary reflections which would enable us to say without qualification, *that* (referring to some precisely specifiable
set of phenomena) is Hinduism, Buddhism, Christianity or
whatever. Rather, within each of these broad (and by no
means clear or necessarily exclusive) categories, there are
successively smaller divisions (Vedantic and Tantric; Hinayana
and Mahayana; Shi'ite and Sunni; Catholic and Protestant),
until eventually we come down to the individual and find an
almost person to person variation in belief. Cantwell Smith
has pointed to this 'further fact (i.e. further to inter-religious
diversity) of diversity within each tradition'.[26] Every faith, he
says, 'appears in a variety of forms',[27] to the extent that 'it is
no longer possible to have a religious faith without *selecting*
its form'.[28] Focusing on Christianity in particular, he suggests
that the modern Christian faces a situation – within his own
faith – of 'open variety'[29] or 'optional alternatives',[30] in which
he must come to a decision regarding what form his commitment is to take, rather than assuming that this is something
which is automatically settled simply by his being a Christian
in the first place. Under the general heading of 'Christian' –
and the same goes for 'Hindu', 'Buddhist', 'Muslim' etc. –
there are many possible outlooks which can be taken. In a
sense, each of the mirrors in the hall of mirrors leads off into a
hall of mirrors of its own. Indeed, we may suppose that
Cipher has many fictional first cousins each engaged in a
similar quest to his own – Christians, Hindus, Muslims and
Buddhists who, within the confines of their own particular
faith, are trying to decide where, precisely, to locate their
individual commitment and what to make of those surrounding alternatives to the choice they finally arrive at. We might
think of Cipher as being one stage behind these first cousins,

for he has not yet narrowed down the area of choice into the slightly more manageable bounds of a single particular religion. Although Cipher may, from time to time, cast an eye towards the progress of these first cousins, it must be stressed that his problems, although similar, are *not* the same as those posed by religious plurality for commitment within a Christian or Hindu or other particularized setting.[31]

The fourth point which I wish to mention about the hall of mirrors is, simply, that not all of its reflective surface will bear images of the same size and intensity. It seems likely that the 'adequate accounts' of the world which may have been offered by the various 'dead' religions will not constitute such significant reflections as those offered by the great world religions which are still very much alive today. Similarly, the various localized religions which still flourish around the globe, different forms of tribal animism for example, may be supposed to exert a less potent force than that emanating from the more international faiths. Moreover, according to Cipher's personality, his likes and dislikes, some mirrors will exert a stronger fascination than others.

Fifthly, the religious mirrors must not be seen as straightforward two-dimensional looking-glasses. In one sense, of course, they can be taken as such; for, generally speaking, there *is* a large clearish surface image which announces 'Christianity', 'Hinduism', 'Islam' or whatever to the observer. But simply to stop before such images and to proceed no further would be to take a superficial and ultra-literal view. The mirrors consist of groups of individual believers, and really to see what the images of 'Hinduism' or 'Buddhism' or 'Christianity' offer, in terms of the peace of mind which he is looking for, Cipher must try to see how such committed individuals, who term themselves 'Hindus', 'Buddhists' or 'Christians', see the world. He must try to move from the point of view of external observer, standing outside and looking at superficial pictures of religions, to the perspective of internal observer who is in a position to share more closely the outlook of those who have made a world decision and align themselves to, and so help to constitute, a particular faith. In short, his focus of interest in the religious hall of mirrors will be more on *persons*, rather than the abstract religious systems within which they might happen to stand. For, at the end of the day, it is the lives and thought of individuals who claim to have found some curative response to the sense of lostness which they and Cipher feel, which constitute the particular area which he wishes to investigate.

The sixth and last point about the hall of mirrors simply has to do with the implications both of 'hall' and 'mirror'. These ought, I think, to be made explicit, since part of my reason for choosing this metaphor was because of what they suggest. 'Hall' can mean either the main room of a great house or a passage through which one passes to one's destination. It is important to remember that, though Cipher may feel he is at the outset of his search, he may, in a sense, have reached his destination already. Perhaps his investigative journey will merely involve a change of perspective, so that the passage is seen as the room he wants to get to. This is a point which I will return to in a later chapter. 'Mirror', on the other hand, is derived from the Latin, 'to wonder at', and serves as a useful reminder of the importance of wonder as a basic religious sense.

As well as the objection that in looking for some sort of peace of mind in the various 'adequate accounts of the world' apparently offered by the religions, Cipher is in fact seeking something which simply does not exist, there is also the complaint or caution that, unless he is very careful, he *may* end up focusing his attention on abstractions which have little to do with the varieties of faith by which men and women have actually responded to the human situation. Wilfred Cantwell Smith has argued that:

Neither religion in general nor any one of the religions . . . is in itself an intelligible entity, a valid object of inquiry or of concern either for the scholar or for the man of faith.[32]

According to Smith's analysis, the concept 'religion', and the various religions subsumed beneath it – Hinduism, Buddhism, Christianity and so on, are all relatively recent Western reifications of personal faith into impersonal ideological structures, which act to misdirect our attention away from the actual lived religiousness of individuals and towards apparently mutually exclusive systems which stand quite apart from each other. The word 'religion' should, argues Smith, be dropped from our vocabulary because it is 'confusing, unnecessary and distorting'.[33] Likewise, since modernity has 'conferred names where they did not exist',[34] terms such as 'Hinduism', 'Buddhism', 'Islam', 'Christianity' and so on ought to be done away with. Smith is not suggesting that what have been called the religions do not exist but, rather, that they exist in a form which is distorted by any attempt to consider them in terms of unitary, exclusive entities subsumable under single headings. In place of religion and religions, Smith argues that we ought to talk in terms of two inter-related factors, an historical *cumulative tradition*, and the *personal faith* of men and women. The use of terms like 'Muslim' and 'Christian', at least as nouns, ought to be abandoned since they impose boundaries where none need in fact exist. As Smith puts it, arguing for their purely adjectival usage:

A man cannot be both *a* Christian and *a* Muslim at the same time. The nouns keep us apart. On the other hand, it is not, I suggest, as ridiculous or fanciful as might be supposed, to ask whether in the realm of adjectives it may not be possible for a man to be both Christian and Muslim at the same time. I for one can understand and countenance meanings for the terms in which not only is this possible, but even in which one could say that to be truly Christian is *ipso facto* to be truly Muslim.[35]

Clearly if the hall of mirrors is perceived as a series of distinct surfaces which can be mapped out in abstract theoretical terms whose reflective areas do not overlap, then it falls foul of Smith's analysis and stands accused of seriously misrepresenting the whole religious realm. If we see Cipher's situation as one in which he faces many unitary images reflected from discrete mirrors which we can term 'Hinduism', 'Christianity', 'Buddhism' etc., then there may indeed be a danger of his quest for peace of mind degenerating into a survey of precisely those aspects of religion which might be least valued by those who profess themselves faithful to some religious world certainty.

I hope that by enlarging and clarifying the nature of the hall of mirrors metaphor I have already allayed any fears that Cipher is going to misdirect his search into an assessment of illicit and simplistic reifications. The mirrors are complex, three dimensional and constituted by the faith of *individuals*, on whom Cipher's focus of attention will be firmly set. This is not the place to embark either on an appreciation or a critique of Smith's thought. My concern is simply to consider those aspects of it which might be relevant to Cipher's situation and which might, perhaps, be considered to constitute a serious objection to the intelligibility of his intended quest for peace of mind. Perhaps we can best sum up the direction in which his criticisms point and show how Cipher does *not* stand with those accused, by developing a rather unsatisfactory metaphor which Smith himself suggests in his influential study, *The Meaning and End of Religion*. Complaining of irreverent and insensitive studies of religion, Smith argues that the scholars concerned

might uncharitably be compared to flies crawling on the outside of a goldfish bowl, making accurate and complete observations on the fish inside, measuring their scales meticulously, and indeed contributing much to a knowledge of the subject, but never asking themselves, and never finding out how it feels to be a goldfish.[36]

Such scholars imagine that there are a series of separate goldfish bowls on which they stick the labels, 'Hinduism', 'Buddhism' and so on and proceed to focus their attention as much on the bowls themselves as on what happens inside them. And when they do look inside, their vision is refracted through the distorting glass of the reifications which they have imposed. Cipher, on the other hand, might be seen as being adrift on the sea of possible world certainties, aware of the various currents and seeing those who call themselves Hindu, Christian, Jewish and so on, voyaging in particular directions. He is less interested in plotting divisions in the ocean than to discover where the various navigational possibilities lead, so that, eventually, he may decide which, if any, to follow.

Whilst accepting Wilfred Cantwell Smith's point that it is misguided to suppose that we can draw neatly exclusive lines around individual expressions of religiousness and proceed to juggle intellectually with 'Hinduism', 'Buddhism' etc. as if they were so many easily graspable entities, I have, however, absolutely no intention of changing my vocabulary accordingly. To excise 'religion' and the names of the various faiths from what follows, would leave many embarrassing gaps which I doubt if even Roget could fill convincingly and which would certainly leave me quite lost for words. Indeed Smith's apparently serious suggestions about removing such words from the language shows a strange insensitivity to the mechanics of linguistic change, which tends to come about through reformed usage rather than instant extermination and replacement. So, although from a Cantwell-Smithian perspective someone might object to the way I talk about religion and religions, I would hope that my intended meanings would not be those which they would, thereby, be seeking to condemn.

I hope that the appropriateness of Cipher's name may now be fully apparent. He is Cipher in the sense of nought or zero, because at this point he feels that his life is without direction. He has made no world decision, he is uncommitted, in a state of world uncertainty. He wishes to search in the hall of mirrors for the possibility of a religious integer to place before his existence, so that his life may take on some value which is not eroded by his sense of lostness. The problem is, just as there are many numbers so there are many religions. He is not sure whether they offer the same or different values or if any of them offer the value which he is looking for. He is Cipher in the sense of code, in that he feels his life is mysterious, that, were he only able to discover the key, he would find a deciphering meaning. Again, the problem is, *which* key? He is Cipher in the sense of being someone insignificant, because he feels lost and dwarfed by the environing immensities of time and space in which the fragile planet of his birth seems scarcely larger than a dust-speck, on which his sense of lostness sometimes seems more appropriate than any scheme of sense.

Cipher may seem to be something of a religious outsider and yet there is, perhaps, a loose sense in which he might be described as being religious. Certainly some comments of Wittgenstein's would seem to categorize him thus. 'The meaning of life,' wrote Wittgenstein, 'i.e. the meaning of the world, we can call God. . . . To pray is to think about the meaning of life . . . to believe in God means to see that life has a meaning.'[37] According to these criteria, Cipher certainly prays – or thinks about the meaning of life, though he does not believe in God, even to the not necessarily theistic extent of seeing that life has a meaning. Whether or not such a meaning exists is precisely what he wants to find out. As we shall see in the next chapter, however, his search in the hall of mirrors for meaning which can offer peace of mind, will share at least some of the more troublesome aspects of an *overtly* religious quest.

2

Information as an Inimical Force

In her interesting study of 'the Way' in the religions of the world, Edith B. Schnapper sets out to show the centrality of this concept in religious thinking, arguing that every religious tradition offers some path designed to lead those who take it towards the sort of destinations envisaged by the writer of an ancient Upanishadic prayer who implored:

Lead me from the unreal to the real,
Lead me from the darkness into light,
Lead me from death to immortality.[1]

To suggest, as she does, that religion and the Way are synonymous and that all the apparent variations in direction in fact lead to the same place, would seem to involve a rather serious underestimating of the diversity of phenomena subsumed beneath the heading 'religion' and it simply ignores the view of scholars like Pietro Rossano who argue that it is, as he puts it, 'scientifically certain'[2] that the ways found within the different faiths are *not* the same. However, though I would question some of her conclusions, Miss Schnapper does make many astute observations in the course of her investigation and identifies correctly several important common landmarks which do seem to be encountered on the routes followed by different religions. Thus in a chapter dealing with the notion of *wilderness*, passage through some form of which seems to be a common phase of 'the Way' however it may be envisaged, she remarks:

It is a well known phenomenon that almost immediately we set out on the religious quest inimical forces, from without and within, suddenly appear.[3]

Two very famous examples come to mind immediately: Jesus' temptation by Satan and the attempts of Mara to lure Siddhartha Gautama, the Buddha, off his meditative path towards enlightenment. Leaving aside the question of their internal or external status, and the question of the extent of their comparability, both Satan and Mara constitute inimical forces whose appearance in the wilderness — whether of actual desert or of meditation — constitutes a threat of potential diversion from the way which is being sought.

The apparently unconditional triumph by Jesus and Gautama over their tempters cannot be expected by the ordinary pilgrim, whose path will follow a rather more circuitous route, full of unwanted delays and detours, which, in the end, will probably leave him some distance from his desired destination. St Paul's lament, 'the good that I would do, I do not; but the evil which I would not, that I do',[4] finds widespread echoes across a wide range of religious settings and is surely a more common outcome of temptation than the triumph of a Christ or a Buddha. Indeed, in his study of *Religious Truth and the Relation Between Religions*, David Moses argues that Paul's 'experience of moral failure (and) his feeling of . . . estrangement, of alienation from the heart of reality'[5] is a fundamental human experience. In similar vein, Aldous Huxley, harking back to a saying of Ovid's, has suggested that every human biography, regardless of whether or not its course is considered to be religious, can be summed up in the words, 'I see and approve of the better things, but I follow the worse'.[6] In other words, I have given in to inimical forces which I am unable or unwilling to resist, I have followed a way at odds with a deeper sense of direction.

Chapter 1 saw the birth of Cipher, the individual set down in the religious hall of mirrors and puzzled about how to decide if he may find there, among the multiplicity of images, some mapping of a way which will provide that peace of mind he seeks, a peace of mind which will act curatively upon those feelings of insignificance, mystery and meaninglessness which punctuate his life and threaten to swamp him with a sense of futility. Whether or not we consider his intended quest in the hall of mirrors — regardless of its reaching a religious or non-religious conclusion in terms of commitment – as in some sense a religious endeavour itself, depends, of course, on how we define this troublesome adjective. Certainly according to the Wittgensteinian criteria mentioned at the end of the last chapter it might in some respects certainly be deemed religious. But whatever we decide about this, it is perfectly clear that immediately he sets out, indeed even as he *contemplates* setting out, Cipher encounters the equivalent of what Miss Schnapper aptly terms 'inimical forces' – forces which would halt and obstruct the path which his situation seems to dictate, i.e. his proposed investigation of the images in the religious hall of mirrors.

Cipher's proposed investigative journey will not contain such epochal confrontations as those between Jesus and Buddha and their tempters, and it may lack something of the action and excitement of the sort of archetypal religious quest found in, say, Gilgamesh's search for immortality – for undoubtedly the hazards he must encounter lack the colour of those met with by this ancient Mesopotamian hero. Not for Cipher the terrible scorpion man of mount Mashu, 'whose terror is awesome and whose glance is death'.[7] Nonetheless, Cipher's quest for peace of mind in the disturbing context of a religiously plural world is an urgent one. The difficulties which seem to bar his path and stand in the way of a successful world decision, of a resolution of his neutrality into some form of commitment, although neither grotesque or picturesque, appear both numerous and formidable. Moreover, the possibility of one's life appearing futile and absurd, or of remaining perpetually in a state of indecision, are not exactly negligible risks.

In a sense, this whole book is concerned with anticipating, identifying and exploring some of the inimical forces with which Cipher may have to contend in the wilderness of neutrality set in a context of multiple choice. In this chapter, however, I will confine my attention to certain restraining forces which seem to come into operation even before he proceeds any further than *contemplating* the religious reflections which surround him.

These forces, which centre round the scale of information

involved, threaten to paralyze any quest which Cipher might embark on even before it begins. They pose the temptation of accepting that the quest is hopeless, thus allowing him to give up before he has got started.

In *Mankind and Mother Earth*, a work which he presents as a bird's-eye view of human history, Arnold Toynbee writes:

Religion is, in fact, an intrinsic and distinctive trait of human nature. It is a human being's necessary response to the challenge of the mysteriousness of the phenomena that he encounters in virtue of his uniquely human faculty of consciousness.[8]

Mircea Eliade, writing in the first volume of his *History of Religious Ideas*, offers a similar diagnosis concerning the inevitability of human religiousness. For the sacred, says Eliade, 'is an element in the structure of consciousness and not a stage in the history of consciousness.'[9] Whether we are, by nature, fundamentally religious animals is not a question I wish to discuss here. Trying to prove that all human beings conform to any particular characteristics beyond the more obvious physical ones is an exercise fraught with difficulty, in a species of such diversity as to crowd the pages of its history with figures as different as Genghis Khan, Mozart, Jesus, Einstein, Michaelangelo, and so on – hence, incidentally, my reluctance to take Cipher as representative of any large-scale group. However, regardless of our final verdict on their absolute truth or falsity, remarks such as those of Toynbee and Eliade do point unwaveringly towards the *massive extent* of human religiousness.

From the anonymous cave paintings which throng the caverns at Altamira and Lascaux and still delight us (aesthetically, if no longer religiously) with their graceful sinuousness and colour, to Mark Rothko's looming empty panels in the non-denominational chapel named after him in Houston; from the millions of Muslims who have made the pilgrimage to Mecca, to the mass suicide (or massacre) of hundreds of the People's Temple sect in Guyana; from the bloodthirsty frenzied dancing of the Indian goddess Kali, to Confucian mores of firm gentleness and poise; from the elaborate opulence of the Hindu temples of Khajaraho, to the emptiness of a Zen garden; from the marvellously named Kurrichalpongo, the aborigines' creator deity, to Milton's Satan; from Gregorian chant to recitation of the sacred syllable Om, humankind has marked out clearly in a multiplicity of different ways and in different mediums its deep concern with the sacred.

But what is all this to Cipher, and why should it constitute an inimical force? The colourful descriptivism of a natural history of religions may provide a fascinating intellectual side-show, but how do the various manifestations of religion actually affect him? I want to keep the focus of attention firmly set on the situation and concerns of my fictional hero, but already it seems to have shifted to a hurried and impersonal glance at some random items drawn willy-nilly from the rich frabric of religious history: clearly a corrective move is needed.

In the previous chapter, listing some of the things which might be found in Cipher's room were he to meet with a suspicious end and so attract the attentions of careful professional searchers, mention was made of a preponderance of books on comparative religion. But among them the searchers might also find works by Amiel, Barbellion, Bashkirtseff, de Guerin and other famous exponents of the art of journal writing. For Cipher will have an interest in the thoughts of others who have pondered deeply on the question of life's meaning and have left behind meticulous records of their experience of the world. Indeed, beside such masters of the genre, it is by no means improbable that the searchers would find Cipher's own writings, a meditative record of his struggle to make sense of things in his religiously plural world, an attempt to come to some point of decision which would release him from his unwanted state of neutrality. As Mircea Eliade says in his own Journal, *No Souvenirs*, which contains autobiographical reflections between the years 1957 and 1969, this type of writing may be 'anything from a calendar to a diatribe, to a table of contents for the next Summa Theologica'.[10] Cipher's writings certainly will not aspire even to the most embryonic Thomistic synthesis. They may, however, provide us with a closer realization of what it would be like to be in the hall of mirrors, of how having access to detailed information about the whole range of human religiousness from the prehistoric to the present could severely complicate the whole issue of personal commitment. By referring briefly to Cipher's imagined writings, we may counteract the threat of his being pushed into the background by a more standard descriptive approach which might eventually lose sight of the dilemma which it set out to investigate. We can, in other words, use an extract from his imagined journal as a corrective device to make sure that the focus of attention remains set on the problems of an individual who is aware of the varieties of possible religiousness but is uncertain which, if any, to adopt himself, rather than letting it shift on to a phenomenological account of the different elements of that awareness.

Cipher writes:

I am dazzled by a glittering mosaic of religious lights, though – paradoxically – I feel as if my eyes are swathed around with a heavy blindfold. All across its surface are numerous rips, gashes, pinpricks of various shape and size. From them issues light of different colour, duration and intensity. Seen cumulatively with my eyes wide open, the effect is confusing, almost blinding. By closing my eyes to a slit and squinting resolutely in one direction, I can imagine what it must be like to see the light through a single aperture only. Searching back in time, history reveals occasions when individuals *were* only conscious of that source of light which was sanctioned by whatever society they belonged to, their path through life was lighted by a single faith – within which there were often huge variations, but beyond whose circle of radiance was perceived no alternative illumination, but only the darkness of denial. No other sources of light were perceived, or, if they were, it was so dimly that they could automatically be rejected as inadequate and inferior. Sometimes I wish that I too existed in so straightforward a context of commitment. But my eyes are wide open and I can turn my gaze in all directions. My view is not seriously restricted by obstructions of distance or ignorance or *a priori* condemnation. Faced thus with a myriad of possible pathways, illumined from a seeming galaxy of lights, I stand undecided, uncertain how, or in what direction, to proceed.

Light pours from the life of Jesus and millions try to walk in the course which it illumines; light pours from the teachings of Gautama Buddha and millions guide their way according to this beacon; the Qur'an burns with a singular intensity which draws submission from millions of Muslims; the wisdom of the Hindu Vedas points a beam which seeks to cut a swathe through the illusions of existence, millions direct their steps accordingly.

Looking across the religious spectrum there is a blaze of luminosity – Christianity, Buddhism, Islam, Hinduism, the light of Jainism and Sikhism, the incandescent history of the Jews, the alluring irridescence of Taoism, the glow of Shinto and the spark of the Parsees. Further off, and dimmed into a subdued glow, the smouldering embers of the dead religions are still just visible, vanished searchlights whose beams once probed the darkness of uncertainty: Aztecs, Egyptians, Sumerians, Dravidians and those nameless tribes before them who trace our history back to the caves where we still find flickering traces of a religious consciousness. Coming up the stream of time again, the new religions of the present provide a cacophany of coloured light, psychedelic, bewitching and fantastic amidst the background illumination of more traditional outlooks which have sometimes lost something of their original sheen.

Is there, from any of this host of sources, a light which can cast its brightness on *my* life? Can I see anything in the light of the world's religions which makes sense of my individual existence, which allows it to be anything other than transient, unimportant, troubled and confused? Or am I simply looking towards a mesmerizing fantasy kaleidoscope which offers nothing but distraction from the uncomfortable truths of the human situation? Am I looking at things the wrong way round, are the religious lights simply blindspots on the fabric of everyday existence which I have mistakenly taken to be a blindfold? Are the different points of light truly derived from some sense-giving 'wholly other' entity or state, or are they simply painted on the fabric of the world, like smiling masks on a frightening face put there by children who are intimidated by the ogres of darkness, pain and death? Ought I to ignore them all, paint over them with realistic colours, accept that I have come of age and that the religious lights have all gone out, that they illumine only our history, tell us something about the past but offer no insight into how we ought to live today? Or is there, somewhere in the glittering array, a thread of truth and meaning which can lead the deepest sense of lostness to the homecoming which it seeks? Does God or Brahman, Nirvana or the Tao, shine through the fabric of the everyday mundane existence that I lead, and, if so, are their several radiances ultimately unitary or irreducibly diverse? Or are such points of blinding light, attested to by thousands who have followed paths lit up by them, merely the cumulative phosphorescence of lives consumed by dazzling illusion?

Thus, as he stands across the threshold of the hall of mirrors, the view so far as Cipher's eye can see is one of dazzling extent and complexity. Such is the range of relevant material open to him that the first inimical force is simply constituted by the *scale* of his informedness. What creates his dilemma *and* seems to frustrate any attempt to resolve it is an awareness, already extensive and capable of massive potential enlargement, of the varieties of human religiousness. The sense of paralysis occasioned by a realization of the vastness of the religious realm, and the attendant difficulties of any attempt to traverse it in the course of an investigative journey, can find expression in two forms, what might be called an *internal* and an *external* sense.

Internally, Cipher may think that he is, quite simply, hopelessly ill-equipped to undertake the work which his predicament seems to demand. For, if he is to make an effective investigative journey through the hall of mirrors, then surely he must be multi-lingual, gifted in theology and philosophy, possessed of a clear historical overview and willing to embark on an extensive programme of world travel – otherwise he may see only the most superficial aspects of the various images which hold him in neutralistic thrall. Whilst he is no dullard, Cipher is no polymath either, and it would go far beyond the bounds even of his fictional status to suppose that he had the necessary powers of perception and retention adequately to survey the whole. It would, of course, be ideal if Cipher *could* understand all that met his gaze, and if his gaze was of sufficient depth and breadth as to be able to encompass the whole range of religious phenomena sparkling before him – but this is simply not the case. Were it imagined to be so we would have moved from very low key fiction to the most exaggerated fantasy. Cipher's powers are limited and his life is short, he cannot hope to understand or to cover everything – even with the help of his whole library of books on comparative religion.

Although the recognition of his limited abilities and the

vastness of the task he must attempt may seem somewhat disheartening, we must remember that Cipher is looking for peace of mind rather than trying to prepare the groundwork for some encyclopedic study, exhaustive in range and unfailing in detail. The problem is addressed to *his* situation, and he must try to cope with it as best he can. To bemoan his lack of skill and − on account of it − to abandon the problem of commitment in a religiously plural world as insoluble, would be to deny that the problem is addressed to him, preferring instead a reading of his situation which sublimates the perplexity he feels in the hall of mirrors into the call for an all-encompassing natural history of religion − something which clearly *cannot* be undertaken realistically by any individual single-handedly and whose point of completion may be almost indefinitely postponed. Cipher is not being asked to produce an encyclopedia but, rather, to make a world decision. The two exercises are not identical. If certain things lie beyond his competence and understanding − as they are bound to do − that is no reason for Cipher to abandon his proposed quest. Such things will simply have to be by-passed as irrelevant. For, if he genuinely cannot understand something, if it is expressed in a language he cannot master and of which there is no translation, or if it involves ideas which he simply cannot grasp, then such a thing would seem unlikely to be able to provide the peace of mind he is looking for. Like Descartes, Cipher must recognize the limitations of his abilities and the briefness of his life − and reconcile himself to getting on with the job to the extent that, as Descartes might put it, 'the mediocrity of his talents' and the 'brief duration of his life' allows,[11] rather than concluding that such mediocrity and finitude provide a valid excuse for not trying. They are important defining features of his problem rather than crippling limitations which mean he can never hope to solve it.

It is rather less easy to avoid the 'external' manifestation of this first inimical force, the worry occasioned by the sheer extent and complexity of the hall of mirrors. Given the huge range of phenomena involved, to what area is Cipher to apply those skills which he *has* got at his disposal? In the time that is available to him, where should he begin his investigation and what course should it follow? Obviously he cannot hope to study *everything*, but, at the same time as acknowledging the inevitable incompleteness of his studies, we would presumably not wish to allow that he may therefore focus on *anything*. In short, if his goal of reaching a decision about commitment in the context of a religiously plural situation is not rendered *unrealistic* by the inadequacy of his skills, then surely it is rendered *impossible* by the extent of the phenomena which would need to be considered.

Perhaps at this point, it may be useful to try to place Cipher in some sort of perspective vis-a-vis the disciplinary area whose work has been largely responsible for facilitating his view of the hall of mirrors in the first place. After all, is it not possible, even likely, that he will find valuable procedural clues about how to approach the immense mass of religious information stretching out before him, within the work of those disciplines which have collected that information and have thus directly fostered the conditions for his troubling awareness?

Cipher's entry into the hall of mirrors has been made possible, very largely, by the work which has been carried out under such subject headings as 'comparative religion', 'history of religion', 'science of religion', 'phenomenology of religion' and so on. I will, for convenience, refer to these variously named endeavours by the single title 'religious studies'. In so doing I am guilty of considerable simplification. However, despite their differences in method and ideology, the several variations occurring, beneath the broad general heading which I am imposing, *may* be considered similar in terms of their outcome in increasing our awareness of the extent and diversity of religions.

The awareness of, and possession of information about, religions in a plural sense may be seen as going through three fundamental stages. We might call these *the three ages of religious studies*.

Firstly, there is a phase of discovery, largely undertaken – or rather occurring – in an undeliberate and somewhat haphazard way. In it occurs the acquisition of information about hitherto unknown areas. Such information is often not

particularly accurate and its acquisition may be quite accidental. This first age lays the initial seeds of an awareness that the
religion with which we happen to be most familiar is not the
only one in the world.

Secondly, there is a phase of deliberate and systematic
investigation of a more definitely circumscribed area. The first
age acts to alert us to – and disseminate initial information
about – the *existence* of new religious phenomena, the second
age begins the process of gaining reliable and detailed knowledge about them.

Thirdly, there is a phase of reflection, which marks a loss of
confidence in the unselfconscious fact-gathering of religious
studies' second age. Questions relating to method now tend to
be given more prominence than those referring solely to
aspects of the material under study.

In these three ages, religious studies tends, respectively, to
display what we might term its *primitive*, *classical* and *modern* forms.

Such a rough threefold model can be applied both to the
study of religion as a broad disciplinary area *and* to an
individual's approach to religions. Indeed, to some extent,
ontogeny repeats phylogeny here – to put it in evolutionary
jargon, the stages of awareness found in individual consciousness mirroring those occurring in the subject as a whole. I will
consider phylogeny first, looking at religious studies in its
primitive, classical and modern manifestations, before turning
to ontogeny and considering how such different forms might
influence Cipher's situation.

In its most primitive form, religious studies (and it is, of
course, doubtful if the name is accurately applicable to much
of this early phase) begins with travellers' accounts of what
appear to the writers concerned as utterly alien and often
damnable phenomena. Leaving aside the embarrassingly fratri-
cidal relationships between the semitic family of faiths, and
talking from a purely Western perspective, if we turn to those
early works of European writers returning from travels in
India or China we can find some good examples of the sort of
outlook primitivism allows.

Thus in William Finch's account of his travels in India in

1608, we find descriptions of sacred sculpture which, in the absence of any understanding of the symbolism involved, perceived them as demonic and disgusting. Finch saw gods:

with long hornes, staring eyes, shagge hair, great fangs, ugly pawes, long tailes, with horrible deformity upon deformity.[12]

As Partha Mitter has pointed out in his fascinating history of European reactions to Indian art, even if we thoroughly searched the Hindu pantheon, 'we would be hard put to find such a monster'.[13] The frequent non-correspondence of description to the actual existence of anything so described is a common feature of the primitive form of religious studies. New things are first conceived of very largely in terms of existing categories, quite regardless of how good a fit they might be, or according to wildly innaccurate preconceptions. Thus the first Western accounts of Eastern religiousness viewed temples as churches, consecrated maidens as nuns and so on, across a wide range of translations which are often understood quite literally by those who encounter them at second hand, such that the illustrators of early travel volumes have come up with some marvellously incongruous pictures. At the same time, stereotype descriptions of monsters and devils, all the dark side of the early Christian psyche, crop up again and again, foisting on the novelties of Hindu iconography an interpretation which had its origin more in the Western sub-conscious than in any observable features of the phenomena concerned. Commentators have spoken of the virtual 'inability of the Europeans to describe a religious system except in Christian terms'[14] and of the way in which early Western observers 'created Hinduism in their own image'.[15]

The often amusing misconceptions of primitivism are gradually weeded out and corrected as the classical form of religious studies comes to assert itself, gradually gathering momentum so that its increasingly accurate collection and cataloguing of religious facts covers an ever wider area. Scholars now talk confidently about a *science* of religion, which will lead unerringly to a clear understanding of the

entire religious realm. Gone is the wholesale rejection of
'other' religions as comical, false or iniquitous – an attitude
common in primitivism. Instead, we find the widespread belief
that, as Max Müller, editor of the *Sacred Books of the East*
series (which were perhaps the literary pinnacle of religious
studies in its classical form), put it:

Every religion, even the most imperfect and degraded, has something
that ought to be sacred to us, for there is in all religions a secret
yearning after the true, though unknown God.[16]

It is realized that the accumulation of sufficient data to
perceive this unknown deity is yet in its infancy, the science of
religion is still only in embryonic form, but no doubts are
expressed about its successful development. Though it may
not *yet* be possible to specify the exact nature of such a
discipline in all its details, classicism is characterized by a
confidence in its own powers to bring about a golden future in
which we will have all the facts about religion and will
understand them perfectly. Thus James C. Moffat talks of
'marking out the ground-plan on which the final structure (of
the science of religion) is to stand',[17] and his two volume
Comparative History of Religions, published in 1875, is
presumably intended to make a substantial contribution to
laying the foundations.

That the ground-plan which Moffat marks out may itself
contain such difficulties of procedure as to prevent any stone
from being firmly laid (or to question the stability of any
eventual edifice which he and like-minded workers envisaged
building on it) is a worry which will only seriously trouble
those in the third age of religious studies when the subject
takes on its modern form. Moffat still belongs to an intellectual milieu where two great world religions may be compared
in a matter of pages and one of them be found wanting.
Whilst in retrospect one may admire the bold strokes of such
intellectual audacity and envy their apparent conclusiveness,
at the same time one realizes that the methodological naïvety
with which they were carried out renders the final result
untrustworthy. The massive structures of classical religious

studies still provide much of the stage upon which the concerns of its modern form are acted out, but it is a stage upon which there are many separate structures and much controversy; it does not bear upon it anything resembling the single, monolithic and triumphant science envisaged by many of those who built it.

The contrast between the mood of classical and modern religious studies may be quickly illustrated by juxtaposing two quotations. The first is Emile Burnouf's famous methodological prophecy which envisages a future for the subject in similar terms to Moffat's, the second is from Ralph Wendell Burhoe's assessment of the current methodological status of the subject.

First Burnouf, writing in 1870:

This present century will not come to an end without having seen the establishment of a unified science whose elements are still dispersed, a science which the preceding centuries did not have, which is not yet defined, and which, perhaps for the first time, will be named science of religion.[18]

Second Burhoe, writing a century later:

It could be said that the scientific study of religion is today in a more primitive state than was biology two centuries ago. We have not yet had our Darwin; we have hardly had our Linnaeus to sharpen our basic descriptive terms and their classifications.[19]

Symptomatic of the growing doubt that such things as Moffat's confidently staked out ground-plan can, in fact, be built on, or that Burnouf's prophecy can ever be fulfilled, we find in the modern form of religious studies much discussion as to whether any sort of clear-cut methodology is possible in this area. The conclusions reached are often pessimistic in terms of allowing the sort of wide-ranging and conclusively answer-giving discipline which classical scholars seem to have envisaged. Schmid sums up something of the mood of modernism when he observes:

As paradoxical as it may sound, the more we know, the less we know. The more extensive and detailed our knowledge is, the greater is the problem and the more reserved are all our statements about religion.[20]

Religious studies in its modern form might, in fact, be characterized by an uncertainty about how to proceed, given the extent of its information about religions. Thus, as early as 1905, Louis Henry Jordan noted with some alarm that a particular difficulty in the study of religions is 'the overwhelming mass of detail, still rapidly increasing, which confronts every investigator'.[21] By 1958, G. F. Woods had realized that 'we are standing near an explosion of knowledge'[22] which has left us somewhat shell-shocked; and, some twenty years later, Eric Sharpe characterized religious studies as involving 'rapidly increasing accumulations of material'[23] in search of some method to make sense of it; whilst, in similar vein, Schmid saw the contemporary situation in the subject as one of 'boundlessly broadening acquaintance with religious data'.[24] It is realized that such accumulation of data is not a satisfactory end in itself. As Bleeker put it, though we have increased our knowledge about religions dramatically, there still remain 'many blindspots on the map of our insight'.[25] There is also a growing awareness of the effect which such information may have on individual religiousness. Frederick Streng, for example, draws attention to the threat which such material poses for the stability of any *particular* faith stance.[26] The picture of modernism which emerges is almost that of a rather dazed band of miners who have accumulated a huge amount of precious ore, yet are unsure just how to process or refine it, and are beginning to realize that it may not be a safely inert substance, but rather that it might exert an almost radioactive potency.

This suggestion of three ages in religious studies, with their corresponding dominant moods of primitivism, classicism and modernism, is intended as a very rough thematic model rather than an accurate historical analysis. In terms of the discipline as a whole, it would not be easy to establish clear chronological watersheds which effectively separated the three ages. We might, perhaps, see the first as extending up to about 1700 or so, the second to the late 1800s or early 1900s, and the third from then until the present. But this crude tri-section of the past ought not to be relied on as anything more than an *indication* of some general features, which a work falling within any of its divisions *might* be expected to display in terms of its perception of a religiously plural world. Inevitably, some works will come 'out of sequence', so to speak, belonging more properly to the intellectual climate of a past or future age. Thus a work belonging chronologically to the third age may, in fact, be more primitive in outlook than a work actually dating from the first age, in which such an outlook might be expected.

Regardless of the historical validity of this crude model (and it is not something which I would wish to present as being much more than a useful device for putting Cipher's situation into context, in terms of giving some idea of the likely evolution of his particular perspective on the religious hall of mirrors) the notions of primitivism, classicism and modernism *are* useful on the ontogenetic level, on the level of *individual* attitudes to religious pluralism. But, again, we ought not to see them as three consecutive stages in a developmental model which everyone passes through uniformly, but rather as attitudes of mind which may be held singly or serially or in unpredictable combination.

Had Cipher been born into the first age of religious studies, and had he displayed all the marks of the primitivism normally associated with it, it would have been impossible for him to have perceived the hall of mirrors in the way in which he does: the information necessary would simply not have been available. The chances are that his situation would have been similar to the one looked back on rather wistfully in the extract quoted from his journal, where only a single source of religious light was visible. Any illumination straying into the visual field of primitivism from other religions would be likely to be seen as faint, and probably fantastic. Something which could not, at any rate, be taken seriously as constituting an alternative.

In so information-soaked a culture as ours it would be difficult to pinpoint precisely Cipher's ontogenetic recapitulation of primitivism, his slowly dawning perception of the fact that there are different religions in the world. In one version of an imaginary biography which we might suppose Cipher to have lived through, his first awareness of the fact that there are 'other' religions in the world could be seen as being mediated via television or newspapers, or through his encountering the visibly different customs of the various religious groups which occur in a multi-cultural society.

Had Cipher been born into the second age of religious studies, and displayed all its typical classical features in his own outlook on religions, then it is more likely that he would have been concerned with pressing ahead and discovering more and more about the religious images in the hall of mirrors, rather than with feeling perplexed by them. On an ontogenetic level, Cipher would pass from a primitive to a classical perspective only supposing that what he perceived, albeit dimly, in the earlier phase was of sufficient interest to him to encourage him to find out more about it. If an interest in what religions say about the world was simply not something he had, then it would, of course, be most unlikely that he would ever engage in the systematic study which is the hallmark of classicism.

Cipher is, however, a typical child of the third age of religious studies and displays all the characteristics of the modernism associated with it. As such, he is deeply perplexed by the information which he has at his disposal about the religions of the world. No longer are the 'other' religions something so faintly perceived and so distant as to constitute a matter for curiosity rather than perplexity. No longer can the information which he gathers about them appear to be an end in itself. He displays what might be taken as the three key features of modernism: extensive informedness about religion; no firm base in terms of commitment to any particular outlook; and an uncertainty about how to proceed.

Let me repeat that it would have been quite possible for Cipher, contemporary though he is, to have had a primitive outlook on the hall of mirrors, with its various images being darkly perceived through the distortions of a religiously xenophobic outlook. Thus, for example, as late as 1939, we find Gervee Baronté writing of Hinduism as a conglomeration of superstitions and myths, full of what she calls 'beastly rites', which, in her analysis, are simply based on a widespread 'sex hysteria'.[27] Any hysteria in her fascinating book, *The Land of the Lingam*, in fact derives, not from the phenomena under study, but from a style of writing worthy of the most retarded primitivism – although chronologically she is writing in the third age of religious studies. There would be many interesting problems to consider were Cipher born into the first or second age of religious studies, or if he displayed a primitive or classical outlook rather than a modern one. However, these are not the settings which I have chosen to explore here.

Ernest Becker has spoken of the useless overproduction of information, and in his interesting psychoanalytic study of our time, *The Denial of Death*, he suggests, echoing Otto Rank, that the man of knowledge is currently 'bowed down under a burden he never imagined he would have: the over-production of truth which cannot be consumed'.[28] In an attempt to see how Cipher might cope with the first inimical force which stands in his way (in its external dimension), that is, the sheer extent of available information about religions, the vast expanse of the hall of mirrors, we have considered how he stands in relation to religious studies – the disciplinary area which has been largely responsible for allowing him access to a perspective of extensive plurality in the first place. Going back to the passage quoted from his journal, the work of religious studies has acted to remove various obscurities of ignorance so that the different religious lights may shine brightly across almost the whole of their reflective surface. It seems clear that, in a sense, Cipher is repeating at an individual level some of the problems which the subject itself now seems to be encountering. For we have seen how scholars belonging to the third age of religious studies are often puzzled about how to cope with the massive amount of information which they have at their disposal. Becker's comment about the useless overproduction of information – even if it *is* true – seems particularly appropriate when we consider the verdict of a writer like Schmid on the key task of present-day religious studies. According to Schmid, that task simply consists of 'finding the thread which leads through the enormity of the evidence'.[29] In the course of this exploration of the hall of mirrors, Cipher will refer to religious studies again for guidance on more particular questions. Clearly, though, as a source of possible advice about how to cope with the sheer mass of material around him, there seems to be no clear advice given: the subject itself is grappling with the selfsame problem.

In terms of Cipher's problematic situation, it may seem as if this attempt to gauge his position in terms of the disciplinary area of religious studies has been rather a wasted effort. After all, it provides no answer to the question of how Cipher is to deal with the external manifestation of the first inimical force to confront him in the hall of mirrors. However, although he certainly cannot, so far, claim to have found any clear-cut methodological guidelines which might have acted to point the way out of his current dilemma, Cipher ought to have derived at least one important clue from this review of some aspects of the disciplinary area responsible for facilitating the view of the hall of mirrors which he sees. Namely, that it is very unlikely that further information by itself will shed much light on the matter. As Bleeker has remarked, information and insight do not seem to be coterminous.

What, then, of the temptation posed by the external manifestation of information as an inimical force, i.e. abandoning an investigation of the hall of mirrors as impossible? What is to stop cipher from looking not only now at the massive extent of the information which constitutes the hall of mirrors, but also at the apparent inability of religious studies to deal with it, and drawing the conclusion that the scale of the problem precludes its solution? Surely now, more than ever, he might be thought to have reason to abandon any quest for peace of mind in the hall of mirrors as inevitably inconclusive – because there will always remain images which he simply will not have time to consider. And if he is fated to deal with only a small part of the hall of mirrors, then why bother unduly about a decision which, given the scale of the situation, is going to have an inbuilt problem of incompleteness, arbitrariness and provisionality?

Just as his response to the *internal* dimension of this problem was very much a common-sense one which accepted his limitations and resolved to get on with the business as best he could, so, I think, must his resolution of the *external* dimension of the problem of information likewise be dealt with in a somewhat rough and ready manner. Cipher must simply deal with the brightest mirrors first, deal first with those images which he finds the most dazzling and appealing, and proceed from there as time and energy, ability and opportunity allow. This is by no means a completely satisfactory answer. It must, however, suffice in terms of getting the job *started*, if not completed.

We might, perhaps, sum up and conclude this chapter – and anticipate something of the next one – by likening Cipher to that most celebrated solver of apparently intractable dilemmas, Mr Sherlock Holmes; for both view information from very much the same practical outlook. Consider, for example, this assessment of his friend by the worthy Dr Watson:

His ignorance was as remarkable as his knowledge. Of contemporary literature, philosophy and politics he appeared to know next to nothing. My surprise reached a climax when I found incidentally that he was ignorant of the Copernican theory and of the composition of the solar system.
'You appear to be astonished,' he said, smiling at my expression of surprise. 'Now that I do know it I shall do my best to forget it.'
'To forget it!'
'What the deuce is it to me?' he interrupted impatiently: 'You say that we go round the sun. If we went round the moon it would make not a pennyworth of difference to me or to my work'.[30]

Whilst I do not wish to subscribe to Sherlock Holmes' theories on learning and psychology which go along with this assertion, much of what Cipher sees in the hall of mirrors would not make a pennyworth of difference to his attempts to reach a world decision. Like Holmes he may, therefore, display a startling ignorance; he is simply not interested in accumulating data as an end in itself, but rather in solving a particular problem, and, as we shall see in the next chapter, this does not require as a pre-requisite an acquaintance with *all* the facts.

At the beginning of this chapter, I contrasted the responses made to temptation by Jesus and Buddha with those of the ordinary individual embarking on some 'Way'. The temptation which the inimical force of information places before Cipher is that of abandoning his endeavour to make a decision about commitment in the context of a religiously plural world, on the grounds that he is insufficiently talented, or that the field is simply too extensive to cover properly. Cipher does not respond to such temptation like a Buddha or a Christ, such that the problem of information as an inimical force is conclusively dealt with. The way in which he does respond to it may be unsatisfactory when measured against some scale of absolute victory, but in terms of the ordinary pilgrim's common (rather than sublime) sense, it has, I hope, the merit of being realistic.

3

The Slap and the Salamander

Cipher's situation – the religious hall of mirrors – has now been roughly surveyed and, in considering information as an inimical force, we have stressed the extent and complexity of this environment. Something of Cipher's own nature and desiderata have been stated too; his situation *vis-a-vis* the disciplinary area of religious studies has been mapped out, and we have seen his common-sense response to what might be called the informational barrier. Cipher is now poised to proceed on an investigative journey among the many perplexing religious images with which he is surrounded, taking first those that make the strongest impression on him and investigating as he may, accepting his limited time and abilities as part of the situation with which he must cope (rather than as a disqualification which prevents him from proceeding any further). Cipher's sense of zero, in other words, one of the strands of meaning in his name which I wish to stress, is ready to explore some religious integers to see if they can offer an acceptable value for his existence.

In another journey, whose course I cannot map out in this brief volume, Cipher might have chosen to survey the various available *explanations* of religion rather than the religious images themselves. For it might well be supposed that the religious hall of mirrors is but a glassy mirage which modern thought has effectively shattered. After all, are there not philosophical, psychological and sociological accounts of precisely those images before which Cipher stands uncertain and mesmerized, which reveal them to be things of no significant substance, about which he ought not to concern himself beyond a purely academic interest? Cannot the existence of God be seriously queried by logic, or the nature of such a supposed entity be shown to be no more than a projected

44

father figure, or a social emanation, or a source of narcotic escapsim in a heartlessly unjust world? Surely such figures as Hume, Freud, Durkheim, Marx and so on have effectively shattered *all* the mirrors which Cipher might look into – and rather than bringing untold years of bad luck for the generations who followed in their steps, they have provided freedom from enslavement to misleading ideas, directing eyes squarely to the realities of the human condition and away from the distracting dazzle of the illusion of transcendence.

If they are accepted as being accurate, such explanations of religion lead unerringly to the conclusion that whatever peace of mind this realm of human experience might *seem* to offer, it is founded on the sand of muddled thinking, illusion or quite contingent societal circumstances, and is, to that extent, unreliable and untrustworthy. Any peace of mind which religion may seem to offer is undermined by an investigation of the *nature* of religion. It pays out counterfeit comfort which will, sure enough, provide a sense of well-being – but only so long as we do not inquire too closely into its origins. Given the possibility that he may not, in fact, be facing an apparent multiplicity of genuine formulae for achieving peace of mind, but rather a set of figures which have been rigged, albeit unconsciously, to provide the sort of answers he is looking for, ought Cipher not to begin with a consideration of those auditing accounts of religion which seek to expose their arithmetic as highly dubious, rather than wasting his time trying to work out which sum, if any, adds up to the right answer?

I do not wish to suggest that the various critiques of religion which explain it in terms which believers would consider destructive, are irrelevant to Cipher's intended quest, or that such criticisms as they level are mistaken. This is simply not an area with which I can deal here – and I will thus offer no opinion as to the truth of falsity of the various explanations of religion which tend to explain it away, acting to erode its foundations as these are perceived by and built on by its believers. At some point in a quest such as Cipher's, attention must, obviously, be given to the various avenues of criticism – philosophical, psychological, sociological – by which we

might approach any religious phenomenon which was considered to be a source of peace of mind. If such a task were
simply ignored, Cipher might well end up accepting something which leads in a Way at direct variance to the directions
desired by that Upanishadic prayer which I quoted at the start
of Chapter 2, that is, which would lead him from the real to
the unreal, from light into darkness. At the stage of his
deliberations to which *these* chapters give access, Cipher's
emphasis will, however, be on asking why those who hold to a
particular religious outlook accept it as a source of peace of
mind. His primary interest will be on the explanations *which
they themselves would offer or accept* for their so doing, not
on causative accounts of why they happen to think and act in
the way they do. To contrive a very simple example: suppose
someone told Cipher that Hinduism provided them with
peace of mind, such that their feelings of insignificance,
mystery and meaninglessness received an adequate, sense-
giving antidote through, say, devotion to the goddess Kali. In
reply to the question *why* they believe such devotion offers
peace of mind, *why* it is curative of a sense of lostness, the
Hindu might reply that their belief is based on that most
ultimate of experiences, the identity of Brahman (the world
soul) and Atman (the individual soul), and the realization that
all else is illusion, a perspective on things which they find
effectively afforded via the mythology and symbolism of the
cult of Kali. In reply to this same question it might also be
replied that they are Hindus because they were born into a
community where what Peter Berger calls 'the cognitive
majority'[1] held similar views, where adherence to such views
receives strong peer group approval and divergence from
them strong disapproval, or where the peace of mind offered
by such devotion as they display only offers some small nectar
of comfort in the rather bitter surroundings of urban capitalist
Calcutta, but that it would disappear in a sweeter social
environment as simply being unnecessary. Cipher's attention
will be set firmly on investigating answers of the former sort.

So, rather than considering the various explanatory
accounts of the origin and nature of religion, accounts which
would almost inevitably act to dismantle the whole structure

of the hall of mirrors as a locus which legitimately offers 'answers' of the sort which interest him, Cipher's *first* steps will be concerned with seeing the various images as they appear to those who do accept them (whether at face value or not) as somehow providing peace of mind.

This may well be the wrong way to tackle things and it may be objected that Cipher is making very heavy weather of a matter which could be solved comparatively simply – in a sense just by looking behind the mirrors and seeing that there is something non-religious there creating the perplexing picture. Presumably this sort of objection *will* be made if one happens to take, say, a Freudian or Marxist view – or if one believes that logic has already demolished such ideas as God even before we reach for our empirical guns. To some extent, Cipher's choice of initially focusing on the religious images, as they are perceived by those who accept them as genuine, is simply a choice. It is one way of doing things, a possible response to his situation, not necessarily the best one and certainly not the only one. It is, however, the one which I, as his creator, have chosen to dictate and which I wish to explore – and in a sense that is justification enough; it simply has to do with setting reasonable bounds to a particular inquiry. However, were such a choice to need further justification beyond fiat, it might be pointed out that for all the destruction which the various critiques of religion seem to have wrought, if we bother to pick up the apparently shattered religious images in the aftermath of some particular attack, it is often difficult to piece together anything which anyone would seriously accept as a picture of religion as it is held to and practised by believers. As Leszek Kolakowski has remarked,

More often than not the philosopher discusses problems which, though perfectly valid in themselves, are very remote from the real worries of . . . religious people.[2]

The philosopher is not alone in preparing intrinsically interesting but rather off-target critiques, psychological and sociological efforts too often seem wide of any mark which a believer would recognize as characterizing his faith. It seems clear to a post-Cantwell Smithian perspective that at least some of this inaccuracy comes as a result of aiming at cumulative tradition and claiming to have 'hit' personal faith.

In view of the apparent refraction which occurs when the critical consciousness encounters religious belief, with a deflection of its subsequent critique on to imagined rather than actual targets, it might be argued that as an essential first step, Cipher must get clear on the nature of the images which perplex him *as they are actually perceived and held to be of value and authority by those who subscribe to – indeed who make up – the various religious mirrors*. For until he has seen clearly how they are accepted as offering peace of mind by those who accept that they do act in this way, he will, in a sense, not really know what he may be accepting or rejecting when he comes to make a decision, either about them or about some critique of them which he might consider in the future. Moreover, the explanations of religion offered by Freud and Marx and the criticisms put forward by philosophy are, almost invariably, directed to a monotheistic type of religion. But many of the images in Cipher's hall of mirrors are not even *theistic*, let alone subscribing to a *single* deity. It is by no means clear if a Freudian critique of religion would apply to Buddhism, or if Hume's superbly crafted critique of the design argument would be applicable to a conception of the world as mayic or samsaric – before such questions can be answered we need a clear view of what the religious images in question involve. This is not, incidentally, to cancel criticism from the syllabus of Cipher's quest, but rather to postpone it to some place outwith the scope of this particular book.

Attempting to see clearly how people accept the religious outlooks they do as offering peace of mind *could*, of course, be a lifetime's endeavour. Cipher could use this point of focus to transmute his search for an answer into a situation where the search itself became, if not the answer, at least the excuse for never arriving at one. Phenomenology could displace and deaden perplexity as he strove to discover in minute and exhaustive detail what makes someone a Hindu or a Buddhist or a Christian, gradually forgetting, in the course of his research into the way in which they accept these religious images as peace-of-mind-offering entities, that in fact he set out to get more than just a super-accurate description. He might well come to a quite brilliant understanding of the history and mythology of, for example, Hinduism: but, in so doing, he may move little closer to a decision as to whether or not he could commit himself to a Hindu view of things. In a sense, information once more exerts an inimical force, this time threatening to draw Cipher into that situation where, in effect, he would be left constructing a full-scale replica model of the religious landscape which he really only wished to map and pass through, and for the purposes of his particular journey, as we shall see in a moment, a fairly simple map will suffice. Information here offers the temptation of deferring decision indefinitely, in favour of complete description. And Cipher, a child of the third age of religious studies, has at his disposal an accumulation of sufficient material such that this kind of painstaking reconstruction *might* be attempted.

As the French diarist Amiel put it, summarizing an obvious but sometimes overlooked truth:

The man who insists upon seeing with perfect clearness before he decides, *never* decides. Accept life and you must accept regret.[3]

Cipher has already come to terms with two regrets: namely, that his abilities are far from perfect, that he has by no means the ideal intellectual equipment to carry out his quest, *and* that the extent of the information and the briefness of his life mean that there will always be a sense in which his search will be incomplete and any conclusion reached incurably provisional. Now he must come to terms with what may be seen as another regret: that for any *particular* area of investigation he cannot wait for *complete* description (which is, after all, never really complete) before making a decision. Given the briefness of his life, the immensity of his task, the limitations of his abilities and the urgency given to his desire to reach some decision about commitment stemming from his sense of lostness in the world, he cannot hope to arrive at a conclusion if he attempts some sort of exhaustive study of every aspect of those parts of the hall of mirrors which he *does* have time to focus on.

Fascinating though they might be, and important for understanding the way in which the religious images are seen by those who accept and help to constitute them, Cipher cannot embark on elaborate explorations around the vast circulatory systems which channel the life-blood coursing through each religious body. Granted that, if he did, he would reach many vital organs, see how the various religions held together as living wholes, feel himself carried along by their vital energies, and so on. Such a wide-ranging exploration would, however, be ill-suited to solving his particular dilemma. He must seek some means of getting straight to the heart of the matter, ruthlessly pushing aside scores of phenomena as being various degrees of periphery, which will only be of real interest to him if the central core about which they orbit is sound.

Cipher's main concern in exploring the religious images in the hall of mirrors is, of course, to establish if he can accept any of these images, in whole or in part, singly or in some kind of combination, as offering peace of mind, as providing some adequate response to those feelings of insignificance, mystery and meaninglessness which trouble him. In this phase of his exploration, which is focused on religion as it is perceived by religious believers, the key question which he will use to steer his inquiries towards the heart of the matter will simply be to ask of the Hindu or the Buddhist, the Muslim or the Christian: 'What makes you profess this faith, on what grounds does your acceptance of it as a legitimate source of peace of mind rest?' Alongside his desire to find out in what way they hold a particular religious outlook to offer peace of mind, is the more urgent desire to find out *why*, in their own terms, they do so. In this way Cipher hopes to drive towards the linchpin of the whole religious structure, that point which the believer would regard as of crucial importance, such that, were it discredited, his faith – if continued – would be in some sense radically changed or devalued. Of such linchpins, which hold together the whole weight of the various images which dance before him in the hall of mirrors, Cipher will seek to ask: 'Is it true? Can I accept it?' If he can, *then* the whole structure which depends upon it will become worthy of extensive – if not exhaustive – study. If he cannot, if a linchpin is found to be in some sense faulty or illusory, or if it remains imperceptible, then the image which depends upon it may be dismissed, *not* as something of absolutely no value (that would be a ridiculous and simplistic over-reaction) but as something which will no longer be of such first-order interest to Cipher as a potential source of peace of mind.

It may, of course, be objected that Cipher's intended focusing on religious images as seen from the inside will end up doing worse violence to the pictures of Christianity, Buddhism, Islam and so on than any external critique, if he brushes some phenomena aside as peripheral and tries to get to some kind of linchpin. This sounds suspiciously like the crudest separation into essence and manifestation. But Cipher is not denying that all religious phenomena contribute to an overall, cumulative sense of meaning, deeply embedded in cultural and symbolic forms. Rather, he accepts that *each* phenomenon is important in as much as it provides access to, constitutes a doorway opening towards, and is expressive of that which gives the whole structure life. This is *not* to say that every religious phenomenon is *similarly* grounded in some originative life-giving experience. Clearly the twentieth century lay-Buddhist preparing a children's life of the Buddha and a close disciple of Gautama are likely to stand at somewhat different distances from the arterial system of Buddhism. In the same way, the nominal present-day Christian, whose religion finds little expression beyond Sunday church going and formal rites of passage at birth, marriage and death, would seem to be located nearer the periphery of this faith than, say, St. John of the Cross. Both they and he will give access to the same originative source of authority which provides final sanction for the outlook they variously adhere to, but, in terms of the analogy with the circulatory system, in one case we are at the very extremities of the body, in the finest of the capillaries, in the other we are nearer to a strong source of pulse. Cipher is assuming that if contact with this pulse is finally broken, or if the heart of the matter turns out to be other than it is perceived by the believer, then the status of their outlook as offering legitimate peace of mind must be questioned. Within any particular expression of religiousness, Cipher will look for the channels which link it to the heart and attempt to work his way back towards it.

Now, of course, Cipher is likely to receive many different types of answer to the question: 'Why do you accept this particular image?' (or, conversely, 'What would make you reject it?') as a legitimate source of peace of mind. The linchpin of a religious outlook as it is perceived by someone who accepts its vision of the world, may be voiced by them as being pragmatic – 'I accept it because it works' (and would reject it if it stopped working); traditional – 'I accept it because countless others have done so in the course of a long and venerable history'; situational – 'I accept it because I know of no other way' (things might be different if I did); or absolute – 'I accept it because it's true' (and would reject it if it were found to be otherwise). I take it as axiomatic that Cipher could not accept something as a curative formula for his troubled mind, for his sense of lostness, if he knew it to be false, or indeed if it was founded on a linchpin which could continue to function independently of the truth – that would be like accepting as a cure for malaria something which in fact left all the symptoms unaltered. He will focus his attention on answers which make reference to an absolute linchpin, not on those of a pragmatic, traditional or situational nature which would not take him to the heart of the matter nor provide a conclusion. For he might quite reasonably continue his questioning in the face of the answers which they offer: *Why* does such and such an outlook work? *Why* did previous generations believe it? Unless he is to be led into some sort of ultimately self-destructive circularity, reference must be made to something else. Cipher's focus *will be on that something else*, the originative, absolute justifying point which explains why a believer accepts a particular outlook to be valid and *in the face of which it would be inappropriate to ask further, 'Why do you so believe?'*

Cipher's attention will, then, be keenly focused on the linchpin of those actual experiences which, in most attempts to justify faith in a particular religious structure, will be referred to as the final authoritative element. Once he has located such linchpins, he will have to try to decide for himself whether or not they are as they are presented and relied upon, whether they are trustworthy as possible foundations for peace of mind. Cipher will not be asking of Hinduism or Buddhism or Christianity, 'Is it true?', but rather, 'On what is the faith acceptance of individual Hindus, Buddhists and Christians ultimately founded?' and 'Can that linchpin of their faith be accepted in the terms in which they present and understand it?' To ask of Hinduism, Buddhism or Christianity 'Is it true?' or 'Can I accept it as a peace of mind offering entity?' is somewhat simplistic and naïve, given that beneath these undoubtedly misleading headings there is gathered such a multiplicity of things. Cipher is concerned, rather, with the basis on which individual believers found their faith, and sooner or later this will, inevitably, take him towards a focus on some form of religious experience. For, as R. C. Zaehner put it:

If religion is to have any meaning at all [and Cipher accepts that it does, though he is not sure of what type or whether it will suffice to give meaning to *his* existence] there must be an element of experience in it: there must be some apperception of what, for want of a more precise word, we must still call the divine, the holy or . . . the numinous.[4]

I agree with Zaehner on our lack of a precise word for the object of religious experience. However, I think 'transcendent' lacks the theistic overtones of 'divine', 'holy' or 'numinous', so I shall use that term instead of the selection which he offers.

By the rather contentious term 'religious experience', I simply mean that which constitutes the internal explanatory root of the phenomena which go to make up a particular religious outlook on the world, i.e. the sense-giving explanation of his beliefs which might be offered by a believer, that which, so to speak, gives life to his faith – such that the diverse phenomena which go to make up a Hindu or a Buddhist or a Christian outlook on things cohere together as organic wholes, their existence ultimately claiming whatever life-force they manifest from an experiential core, variously named God, Brahman, Nirvana, the Tao, Allah etc. This life-giving experience of the transcendent – which extends throughout the religious realm, though it underlies different phenomena at vastly varying depths – seems to be the ultimate internal validation for religion as a source of peace of mind. It is this sort of experience which provides the linchpin which holds together the various images in the hall of mirrors; it is the heart of the matter which Cipher hopes to reach.

Buddha, Zoroaster, Jesus, Muhammad, the writers of the Vedas, Lao Tzu – all provide examples of individuals who have had religious experience of such power and vitality as to leave each generation since them struggling to find an adequate way of putting it into words and action. Such interpretations have been many and various and constitute the major part of the history of religion. But though they may have held sway for years and influenced the lives of millions, no single interpretation has seemed entirely satisfactory, to the extent that succeeding ages are left theologically replete and silent. On the contrary, the religious experience of the great holy men of history, at once both ineffable and generative of seemingly continual interpretations, seems to provide an inexhaustible quarry of *possible* understandings. Such experience stands at the root of centuries of religious practice and gives it the sense it claims. No matter how explicit the doctrine, no matter how tangible the edifice, every religious phenomenon seems to recede (in terms of meaning) to a central and apparently irreducible opaqueness which may be termed 'God' or 'Brahmnan', 'Nirvana' or 'the Tao', and within that opaqueness the heart of religion seems to beat in an endlessly recurring rhythm of systolic ineffability and diastolic attempts at expression and understanding, its pulse apparently generating that situation of diversity, at least in much of its intra-religious sense, with which Cipher is concerned – as we shall see further in Chapter 5. It is towards that heart that Cipher wants to proceed, since it seems that only according to the nature of its pulse can a decision be reached about the quality of life which spreads through its arterial system, offering a structure which purports to give peace of mind. If the religious heartbeat does indeed stem from a genuine encounter with some transcendent state or entity, then its reverberations *may*, perhaps, lull all Cipher's disquiet to sleep. If, on the other hand, that pulse is merely an echo which we have imagined from straining our ears too long in a wilderness whose emptiness, silence and meaninglessness appals us, or if it is the drumming of mere wishful thinking, then Cipher may quit the hall of mirrors and let his search take other directions.

Given this experiential linchpin, Cipher will be relatively unconcerned with the extremities of the religious body. His immediate task must be to get as close as is humanly possible to the heart, or at least to some strong source of pulse, and to *listen* with all the attention he can muster.

However, this source may well seem quite unreachable. If, for instance, he finds he is referred back to the experience of some single historical figure, it may be located in the distant past, and between it and Cipher may stretch centuries of partial deafness and dubious interpretation. But although we may look to them for its classic and defining instances and for the provision of some sort of specialized vocabulary or set of reference points, religious experience is by no means confined to these key figures of the major traditions. Accordingly, there is no reason for Cipher's investigation to be confined only to them. The religious experience of the ordinary man in the street may leave little imprint on recorded history (whether because of its lesser power or his reticence or inarticulateness in dealing with it), but its occurrence may well blaze its way indelibly, if privately, across the path of his own biography, and it certainly serves to re-invest traditional accounts of such experience with an aliveness they could not hope to have were it located *solely* in an unrenewable culturally remembered past. It is towards such incandescent *present* moments that Cipher will direct his inquiries. His interest will be in the point of ignition rather than the subsequent flames, and he will assume that those flames would long ago have been extinguished, or at least have faded, were there but a *single* point of ignition at some historical moment of beginning, which, thereafter, never sparked out again.

Such an assumption receives strong backing in David Hay's *Exploring Inner Space*, a book which attempts to assess the extent of religious experience in modern British society. Hay writes:

What is unique to religions is that they always assert the possibility of getting in touch, directly, with whatever is ultimately 'real'.[5]

Such a getting in touch with what is variously taken to be ultimately real is, I think, what gives religions the peace-of-mind-offering status which they display and which scientific and humanistic alternatives often seem to lack. As J. C. A. Gaskin recently put it:

most religious experience can be described in terms of an awareness of something other-worldly *in relation to which man finds his greatest joy and peace*.[6]

Readily acknowledging the 'decay of [many] publicly available symbols of religion',[7] Hay focuses attention on what he calls 'the sacred dimension to human experience which is prior to all symbols'[8] and without which it might be argued that 'all other dimensions of religion are emptied of meaning'.[9] His conclusions are startling for those who might imagine that in the twentieth century we have become secularized to the point of denying the existence of the transcendent altogether, or of allowing only the very *faintest* 'rumour of angels' any credence. Thirty-six per cent of the sample of people approached by National Opinion Polls answered affirmatively to the question: 'Have you ever been aware of or influenced by a presence or power, whether you call it God or not, which is different from your everyday self?' 'On that basis,' remarks Hay, 'We can predict that about 15 million adults in this country would say the same; that is to say, over a third of the population aged 16 or over.'[10] Similarly, thirty-one per cent of the sample responded positively to the question: 'Have you ever felt as though you were very close to a powerful spiritual force that seemed to lift you out of yourself?' Hay concludes his careful and interesting study by suggesting that:

Probably a majority of the more intelligent, saner and socially responsible people in our secular nation would claim, perhaps rather shyly, to have had these experiences. They may fear they are in a minority, and will be thought by most people to be stupid or mentally unbalanced; but they are merely claiming the kind of contact with ultimate reality which lies at the heart of Western culture and of every great historical culture.[11]

Unless Hay's results are *altogether* wrong, it would seem clear that Cipher's focus on religious experience need not be restricted to a handful of historical cases which may lie so far beyond the reach of effective investigation as to guarantee an 'open' verdict. Moreover, in justifying his location of the linchpin of a religious image in this sort of experience, it would seem quite plausible for him to argue that, were this 'contact with the heart' actually *severed*, were this experiential spark to be extinguished, the status of religion as offering peace of mind would then be vastly diminished. If Hay's exploration of inner space had perceived no confirming echoes in modern consciousness of the ecstatic shouts of the ancients, if no religious outlook today could claim some sort of *direct* unmediated contact with some absolute point of ignition and confirmation, then it might surely be supposed that the hall of mirrors would simply have become misted over, so that it would cease to be the perplexing place which Cipher finds it to be.

Cipher's focus will not, therefore, be on those religious persons whose reference to an experiential basis for their outlook is a second or third hand *referring back*, but on those for whom it is immediate. This is not to say that the faith of the individual which is founded on purportedly direct personal experience of the transcendent is superior to that founded on trust that someone else has experienced the transcendent, or trust in some recorded, historically distant, moment of revelation – they simply offer Cipher a quicker way of getting to the heart of the matter and therefore making a decision about commitment.

A focus on religious experience may also provide Cipher with a basis on which to *begin* to answer the question of the extent to which the different religious images are the same and the extent to which they are different; or the points at which they converge and where, subsequently, they become so divergent. Is there one uniform experience being interpreted variously, or are there various similar but different experiences eliciting a range of descriptions which merely look like a series of interpretations? It is self-evident that at a surface level the different religions *are* different. But does the difference run uniformly from the outermost periphery to the innermost heart? Can we locate any *underlying* similarity which might act to qualify any subsequent difference as secondary and relatively unimportant, or are the different images in the religious hall of mirrors underlain for all their depth with the same differences which so blatantly and problematically characterize the faces they show the world?

Of course, even if Cipher *could* establish that all the different religions had, ultimately, the same experiential source, this would not end his dilemma – though it *would* make it a little less complicated. Firstly, he would still need to know if such a source provided a reliable foundation for achieving peace of mind and, secondly, he would have to decide which of the still different routes to follow towards it. As the Abbott of a Zen Buddhist Priory in Northumberland – who acknowledges the *underlying* similarity of different faiths – put it:

I get rather tired of people telling me that all the ways are the same. They are spectacularly *not* the same. If you want to travel to the priory from the South coast, it does not make much difference whether you go via the M5 and M6 or around London and up the M1. But you must make up your mind and stick to it. If you make a mistake and end up in Cornwall then you reassess the situation and start again from there. Too many people like nothing better than going round and round 'spaghetti junction' in the Midlands, admiring all the roads that lead off from there, but never going any further themselves.[12]

In a sense, of course, Cipher is circumambulating a kind of spaghetti junction in the hall of mirrors. The problem is, he is not sure if the roads go where the signposts say they go, or if their destinations are, in the end, the same. His immediate concern must be to investigate the claims of travellers who say they have been there, to try to decide if the routes they recommend really follow the contours they claim and offer the perspectives they say they have seen. Cipher does not want to end up wasting time and energy disappearing down some blind alley, which in fact leads nowhere, or which may simply go round in a wider and less honest and obvious orbit than that of his spaghetti junction of informed and inquiring neutrality. In a sense, he will seek to go a little way with those travellers who seem to follow the fastest and most direct route, questioning them carefully and subjecting their reports to the closest scrutiny, before deciding if he wishes to make any of the journey at all. And to reiterate the point that he is not interested in *everything* in the religious realm, we might note that he will accept without question all kinds of claims about the quality of the vehicle and the fellow travellers; he accepts that there is much of worth in any religious community in terms of, for example, various social and aesthetic parameters, but *his* question remains: does the road lead to legitimate peace of mind?

'Man's religiousness', as Willard Oxtoby rather clinically put it, is 'a response to a stimulus commonly called "the sacred"'.[13] Joachim Wach, echoing John MacMurray and using the same terms as Oxtoby, has complained that 'a great deal of our modern study of religion attempts to give an account of a response without any reference to the stimulus'.[14] It is the *stimulus*, as the validating source of the various religious responses which perplex him, on which Cipher will try to focus his attention. This does not mean, incidentally, that he will abandon natural theology in favour of some revelatory source of authority. For religious experience can easily be taken as part and parcel of the natural phenomenon of religion, as a common feature of it which can be observed and studied in a manner which makes no *a priori* assumptions about its nature.

The emphasis of Cipher's quest on the stimulus or stimuli behind the religious responses, on the linchpins of those massive religious structures which purport to contain peace of

mind and which together constitute the hall of mirrors in
which he is situated, can be memorably expressed by referring
to a passage from the autobiography of Benvenuto Cellini, a
passage which will, I hope – and you may think at long last –
explain as apposite the otherwise rather odd title of this
chapter. In Book One, Section 4, Cellini relates the following
incident:

When I was about five years old my father happened to be in a
basement chamber of our house, where they had been washing, and
where a good fire of óak logs was still burning; he had a viol in his
hand and was playing and singing alone beside the fire. Happening to
look into the fire, he spied in the middle of those most burning flames
a little creature like a lizard, which was sporting in the core of the
intensest coals. Becoming instantly aware of what the thing was, he
had my sister and me called, and pointing it out to us children, gave
me a great box on the ears, which caused me to howl and weep with
all my might. Then he pacified me good humouredly, and spoke as
follows: 'My dear little boy, I am not striking you for any wrong that
you have done, but only to make you remember that the lizard which
you see in the fire is a salamander, a creature which has never been
seen before by anyone of whom we have credible information.' So
saying, he kissed me and gave me some pieces of money.[15]

Transferring the imagery of Cellini's story to the hall of
mirrors: religious experience is cast in the role of the salamander, and the various interpretative and expressive words
and actions which have sprung up around its sighting are cast
in the role of the slap – as reminders, often systematized into a
formal corpus of ritual and doctrine, of what Eliade terms
'hierophany', that is, what is taken to be an irruption into our
present experience of the transcendent.[16] The salamander is
the internal validating source without which the slap ceases to
have the meaning which it was intended to have (which is not
to say that it would have no meaning at all if the salamander
turned out to be in some way unreal or illusory). Cipher's
emphasis will be on the salamander rather than the slap,
though obviously his approach to it will be mediated through
careful study of the various mnemonic forms which are
immediately visible and accessible to him. Thus, for example,

Cipher will only be marginally interested in the forms of ceremony, the artefacts used, the sacred places etc. involved in worship. His attention will be focused, albeit *through* these secondary phenomena, on the experience which lies behind an act of worship, whether immediately or at some distance, and on which the sense of the worship undertaken ultimately depends. Whereas a student of comparative religion might devote all his energy and attention to an examination of the slap, the *response* to the stimulus of the transcendent, describing its various forms and unravelling its history in terms of various typological categories, Cipher will be more interested in the claimed reality to which prayer, sacrifice, devotion, worship etc. purport to point. As such, he may be breaking the cardinal rule of some scholars' notions of what religious studies is all about (namely, a neutral, descriptive approach which does not get involved and offers no opinion as to the truth or falsity, the authenticity or the illusoriness of the focus of religious phenomena). He will, however, be following a course of action more consonant with his dilemma than 'pure description', however accurate, could ever be.

Just as, had Cellini's father not seen a salamander in the fire, the blow he struck his son would have been pointless in the way in which it was intended, so the various religious phenomena in the hall of mirrors might be dismissed as similarly meaningless, at least in the way that they are intended to be meaningful, were there no experience corresponding to the salamander behind them. Moreover, had Cellini's father been mistaken about what he saw, it is clear that the status of his subsequent action would have to be called into question. There is no point in providing someone with a reminder of what neither you nor they have seen. Likewise, if religious experience is not of what it was originally taken to be, subsequent accounts of it and actions based on it may have to be reviewed. From Cipher's point of view, were there no salamander somewhere in the image at which he looks, then most of what he sees could be dismissed as not constituting the conditions necessary to provide a formula for peace of mind.

This is not to say that religious experience lies immediately and obviously below *every* religious phenomenon. Sometimes the outgrowth of the response, the slap, has moved so far from the stimulus, the salamander, that there is only the most tenuous connection between the two. Indeed one gets the feeling that at some points the response would be distinctly embarrassed to be reminded of its originating stimulus – so uncomfortable might it feel about it that perhaps it would be denied as originative. Indeed much of the various religious structures which Cipher is concerned with would probably survive even a clear-cut proof of the non-existence of their particular 'salamandric' source, though clearly this would change their *tone* of meaning, shifting it from absolute to relative, from metaphysical to social. As such, they might still offer peace of mind, but it would be a somewhat watered-down variety, diluted to the point where it was more an *acknowledgment* of the insignificance, mystery and meaninglessness which craves peace of mind in the first place, than the relationship with ultimate reality which might cure it. Cipher would consider such dilutions only after any remaining full-strength formulae had been considered and rejected.

Nor ought it to be supposed that Cipher's emphasis on the salamander commits him to considering only the most literal interpretations of religious experience. He will follow *any* religious response back to its stimulus in an effort to check its linchpin, in an effort to get to the heart of the matter. Some responses will be more straightforward than others, offering reasonably quick access to a perspective from which the believer's view of the salamander may be seen and shared. Others may seem so far removed from it that they act almost to obscure it from view.

As Lesslie Newbigin put it: 'A study of the eye is useful in its proper place, but it cannot replace the use of the eye for seeing what is to be seen.'[17] Thus in Newbigin's opinion the study of religion might risk being somewhat pointless if 'it is only concerned with the study of the "religious dimension of human experience" and not with the realities which religious experience tries to grasp and respond to'.[18] There are many differing views as to where the focus of comparative religion or religious studies *ought* to put its emphasis – on personal faith or cumulative tradition, on the parahistorical or the historical aspects of religion, or on what Schmid, very confusingly, terms the reality of religion or the religious reality.[19] Newbigin offers another way of putting this stimulus:response /salamander:slap dichotomy. In terms of *his* metaphor, Cipher must try to determine if the religious eyes gaze out on a vista in which some being such as God, or some state such as Nirvana, can be perceived so that the apparent senselessness of human existence is thereby revealed as purposeful by reference to them, or if their field of vision is blank, or focused on some non-transcendent mirage which they mistakenly perceive to be the ultimately real. As to what emphasis the student of comparative religion or religious studies ought to stress, that is an issue with which I am not here concerned.

Some interpretations of religious experience, however, or, to continue in Newbigin's terms, some accounts of the religious vision of things, will *not* be of much interest to Cipher. What J. C. A. Gaskin, looking at the work of figures like D. Z. Phillips and Don Cupitt, has dubbed the personalist theologies,[20] which, incidentally, he sees as being indistinguishable from atheism, will not be of primary importance in his quest. Such theologies offer an interpretation of religion which is so far removed from what most believers take the referent language of their faith to be talking about, that they deposit the stimulus, the salamander, the transcendent – call it what you will – in an abstract theoretical stratosphere, where the religious atmosphere becomes so thin as to be virtually indistinguishable from that of a non-religious understanding of the world and of religion's place in the world. Such interpretations provide no linchpin for the religious structure, they offer no absolute grounding for accepting their particular variety of faith as offering peace of mind. It is one thing to say that the salamander is, in fact, a non-figurative, awesome experience which, in symbolic language, sometimes appears as a mythical reptile, and still to justify the slap (for something memorable has still been encountered); it is quite something else, to found such a reaction on a sighting of what is *accepted* as the death-throes of an unfortunate lizard.

To sum up: in the grand tradition of methodological prolegomena, we have moved very little further forwards. But,
after all, we are *not* concerned at this stage with *following*
Cipher's quest, but with considering what procedural difficulties attend the kind of journey he is planning to make and how
best that journey may be directed. We are at the stage of
route-planning rather than actually going on the journey.

Cipher's focus of attention has been firmly set within the
religious realm: he is primarily interested in discovering how
religious believers perceive their religion as offering peace of
mind, and proceeding from such a vantage point to consider if
he could so accept it. Such a focus could end up as an exercise
in phenomenology, were it not for the insistent stress on the
experiential linchpins of religion which Cipher will make.
Some aspects of religious experience were looked at very
briefly, stressing that this is by no means an uncommon
phenomenon and that Cipher's investigations need not, therefore, be confined to distant historical events which it would be
difficult to approach closely enough for them to provide a
basis on which to arrive at a decision about commitment.
Such a focus may also provide him with a means of determin-
ing how different the various religions really are. Thus we
leave Cipher still standing free of the inimical force of information, and with his proposed investigation of the hall of
mirrors now clearly targeted on the stimulus, the salamander,
which he will seek to *approach through* the more immediately
visible phenomena which constitute the various responses (or
'slaps'). In the next chapter we will begin to consider *how* this
approach might be made.

We should, I think, end on a note of warning – since
Cipher's quest, at least as it occurs within the religious realm,
may simply serve to make him sad (in much the same way as
Michael Novak has argued that religious studies poses this
risk for its practitioners).[21] For, if he can, at the end of the
day, perceive no salamander, no incandescent stimulus for the
religious responses with which he must wrestle, then perhaps
his quest for peace of mind will simply consist of encountering
a number of slaps or body blows which will result in nothing
much more than a severe case of spiritual bruising.

4

Same House, Different Worlds and Inter-Religious Exploration

In 1885, Friedrich Max Müller, editor of the epoch-making *Sacred Books of the East* series and sometimes called 'the father of comparative religion', remarked to one of his house guests who did not happen to share the same teleological views:

If you say that all is not made by design, by love, then you may be in the same house but you are not in the same world with me.[1]

Müller's remark is a reminder that although, of course, we all live in the same world, there *is* a sense, given the apparently different answers found within Hinduism, Buddhism, Christianity, Islam, Marxism and so on, in which it is yet quite intelligible to ask, 'Which world *do* we live in?', and 'Which mode of life and thought is most appropriate in it?' In a situation of plurality as regards world-views, any particular, *exclusive* commitment which does not wish to appear unreflective must, presumably, justify its own outlook as more accurate than any other. Indeed the response of the various religions to an awareness of religious plurality, whether in terms of inclusivist or exclusivist strategies, would make a fascinating study as we move into an era when only the most insular or blinkered of faiths can imagine that it exists in isolation. As Wilfred Cantwell Smith has put it:

The religious life of mankind from now on, if it is to be lived at all, will be lived in a context of religious pluralism.[2]

The time has passed when we could assume that everyone in the same house shared largely the same outlook on the world, such that almost all differences could be accounted for in

terms of the acceptance or rejection of a single particular
view.

The extent to which the new pluralistic context will be
theologically problematic will vary from religion to religion.
It would, for instance, be surprising if it posed exactly the
same problems for Hindu and Muslim alike. Certainly within
the Christian tradition the existence of religions in the plural
is, increasingly, being recognized as an important area of
concern. Cantwell Smith, for example, suggests that the question of how we are to account for the fact of religious diversity
constitutes almost as big an issue as how we are to account
theologically for evil.[3] Likewise, Langdon Gilkey considers
the encounter with other religions to be 'the most important
new issue confronting Christian theology at the present time'[4]
and, intriguingly, he suggests that 'a close encounter with the
nothingness of Buddhism will effect noteworthy changes *in
every recognizable form* of contemporary discourse about
God'.[5]

As John Hick noted in 1973, there has been a Copernican
revolution in Christian theology. Where once Christianity
occupied the centre of a stage and allowed no other actors any
part, except, perhaps, that assigned to them by Satan, the
paradigm shift in thought away from this old Ptolemaic
outlook, with its religiously mono-centric universe, has introduced a host of actors on to a multi-centric religious stage –
though whether they are taking part in the same play, or
addressing the same audience, whether they are written by the
same author or are factual or fictional, remains uncertain.
Hick's account of the massive change in theological thinking
which he accurately *identifies*, assumes too much. For Hick,
the change from Ptolemaic to Copernican theology

involves a shift from the dogma that Christianity is at the centre to
the realization that it is *God* who is at the centre, and all the religions
of mankind, including our own, serve and revolve around him.[6]

Apart from assuming that there *is* a God to revolve around in
the first place, this seems to subsume the various ultimate foci
of the different faiths beneath a single cognomen, 'God'. But

are Brahman, Allah, Nirvana and the Tao accurately reducible to a single principle? Surely this is one of the great
unanswered questions provoked by religious studies.

Interesting though it would be to trace the dawning consciousness within the various different faiths of the religiously
plural context in which they are all so firmly set, to consider
the ways in which their various orbits of meaning may be
influenced by other religious bodies whose trajectories, once
perceived, exert considerable force (whether of attraction or
repulsion), and to explore in general the extent to which the
researches of religious studies influence theologies (and vice
versa), this is *not* the area of concern which I have mapped
out for exploration in this book – though it does, of course,
closely adjoin it and it is useful from time to time to glance in
this direction, if not for inspiration then at least to remind us
of our bearings. For I am not concerned here with how a
Buddhist or a Jew, a Muslim or a Christian resolves whatever
theological dilemmas may be posed by a situation of religious
pluralism, nor with how Buddhist, Jewish, Islamic or Christian theologies react to the information revealed to them by
religious studies. Rather, I am exploring the way in which
Cipher, someone who does not belong to any particular faith,
may, in a religiously plural context, reach a decision about
whether or not to move from a neutral state of mind to one of
particular commitment. Such a religiously neutral individual,
to continue with Müller's terminology, is in the *same house* as
his variously committed neighbours, but in a sense he is in no
world at all – he has not yet decided on how best to view
existence or how to live according to some chosen vision.

There is no question that, as he becomes more informed
about the various alternative views of the world, there is an
increasingly complex problem of evaluation facing the individual who is undecided, who is in a temporary state of neutrality, who has not yet committed himself to any particular
outlook on things, nor yet reconciled himself to a permanent
state of wide-ranging and deliberately chosen agnosticism.
Hindus, Christians, Taoists and so on may all live on the
same mother earth, but the expression which they see on her
face seems, at least at first sight, to be very different indeed.

For the individual such as Cipher, aware of all the different expressions, there is a pressing need for some sort of reliable global physiognomy.

The likelihood is, of course, that someone raised in a predominantly Christian culture will see a more or less Christian expression on the face of the world, whilst a Hindu or Jewish milieu will tend to produce individuals for whom Hinduism or Judaism contain the most accurate reflections of their experience. Likewise, those who grow up in an environment where religion plays little rôle, beyond that of a colourful vestigial survival from what is seen as a more credulous and less technologically sophisticated age, will not, in general, see the world in overtly theistic terms. Obviously this is to simplify and therefore to some extent to distort. Within any cognitive majority there will be dissenters, and depending on the energy of their dissension (itself dependent on many different factors) so the line between majority and minority outlook will waiver and change. Moreover, far from being set at each other's throats, acceptance of some religious outlook and criticism – even rejection – of it, most usually have an at least partially symbiotic relationship, so that the outlook in question is kept vital by the critical consciousness born within it, and the critical consciousness is nourished by a system against which it can develop and exercise its acuity. As Gilbert Murray put it:

Every man who possesses real vitality can be seen as the resultant of two forces. He is first the child of the particular age, society, convention; of what we may call in one word a tradition. He is secondly, in one degree or another, a rebel against that tradition. And the best traditions make the best rebels.[7]

Increasingly, though, we seem to be approaching a time where – at least from the point of view of religion – there is a self-conscious co-existence of so many different traditions that the bloodline of vitality feeds heirs and rebels alike a more puzzling, if also richer, mixture than they could expect from a single tradition existing in undisturbed isolation from serious alternatives to it. It is no longer clear what to adhere to or what to rebel against when trying to come to some sort of decision about religious commitment.

Regardless of what state society or the various religions may or may not have reached regarding the singularity or plurality of their religious self-consciousness, it is clear that, for Cipher, Müller's remark about different worlds sums up and re-states something of the dilemma of the uncommitted individual existing in an uneasy state of informed neutrality, neutrality which knows of many possible roads but is not sure how to decide which, if any, offers the best route in the right direction. In this chapter I will consider how such an individual might go about exploring the different worlds of religious meaning, prior to deciding which, if any, to accept as his own.

I am going to use Müller's comment about how anyone with a different teleology, even if they are in the same house, even if they are standing shoulder to shoulder with him, are, in an important sense, in different worlds, both as a starting point and as a touchstone which will be referred to throughout the chapter. Since the terms 'same house' and 'different worlds' will be heavily used, and in a sense quite beyond what Müller intended in his chance remark, I will begin by explaining the expanded sense I am giving to them here.

The meaning and accuracy of claiming that we *are* all in the same house becomes clear if we reflect on three aspects of life:

First, if we consider the purely physical nature of the world we can see that its basic fabric, according to any human perspective, remains constant across all the flux of personality, time and culture. Light and dark, hot and cold, wet and dry, large and small, animal, vegetable and mineral – such various general categories or states of thing have faced all *Homo sapiens* throughout history (although how these categories are perceived and understood does, of course, vary according to time and place).

Secondly, the basic possible settings for a human life, strung out between its temporal defining points of birth and death, are likewise constant: male or female; childhood, youth, old age; solitude and companionship, poverty and wealth, health and sickness, and so on.

Thirdly, for life lived within these physical, biological and social constraints the same basic structures of feeling obtain: joy, despair, contentment, fear, love, ambition, anger, and so on (though, again, the extent to which these different states are named and articulated may differ enormously from age to age).

In short, what we might call 'the human situation' does not vary appreciably across the centuries. Its basic constituents remain the same for the ancient inhabitants of these islands whose standing stones are the most tangible reminder of their religious presence and for the twentieth century agnostic who may be a knower of many gods and a worshipper of none, and for every other individual spark of consciousness which flickers briefly in the awesomely diverse human multitude before it too (to use a phrase of Thomas Mann's) 'disappears through history's trapdoor'.[8]

That it is, in a similar fashion, metaphorically accurate to suggest – in spite of this basic shared condition – that we are nonetheless in *different worlds*, becomes clear when we consider what might be called the contextual details of specific lives, and when we note the varieties of interpretation put forward to account for life's meaning and to suggest the most fitting ways to live in the light of such a meaning.

By contextual details I mean no more than the particular combination of circumstances in any individual's life – biological, social, cultural, historical, and so on – which serve to render it unique. It is unnecessary to labour the point that within the common area of the human situation, fate, for want of a better word, provides vastly different places in which we must live out our lives. Even individuals born in the same time and culture, indeed even within the same family, may be worlds apart in terms of the course along which their lives and thoughts will run. And when we consider humanity as a whole, the variety of fates is staggering in its unevenness, presenting us with such giddy and unsettling contrasts as that between, say, a Roman galley slave and a concert pianist, a millionaire businessman and a wandering ascetic, between a shaman and a roadsweeper, or an aborted foetus and a man who lives to be a hundred. In this sense we are in different worlds.

However, it is *not* on this sense of being in different worlds that I wish to concentrate here. Why, from the common stock of possibilities, we are dealt such vastly unequal hands, is a question which any religious outlook must face up to in its attempt to provide a sense-giving view of things; but here we can simply include this unevenness of experience among those other common elements which make up the basic human situation, subsuming the dissimilarity it results in individually beneath the fact that it is an unevenness encountered by everyone. The fact of inequality, of difference, is as basic to the human situation as that of love, fear or finitude. As we saw in Chapter 1, it is this fact of inequality or difference, whose apparently random pendulum swings of fortune disrupt so many lives, which plays so important a part in fostering one aspect of Cipher's sense of lostness.

The sense of being in different worlds which is relevant to Cipher's situation and which I do wish to examine here, is that which sets us apart in terms of how we look out upon this world, how we view our situation and how, in consequence, we feel we ought to act in, and understand, whatever particular web of circumstances characterizes our biography.

Again, it is obvious that individuals view the world differently and that consequently they try to live their lives according to different ideal models. This is, after all, what constitutes Cipher's dilemma. Clearly, for the man who considers his situation to be explained largely by the operation of karma and samsara, a different view of things and a different code of conduct will emerge than for one who does not believe in the occurrence of rebirth, but sees himself as a single creation of a personal god of love (rather than the serial outcome of a mechanistic process of moral cause and effect). Or, if the codes of conduct appear to be similar, the reasons behind them will certainly be very different.

Perhaps at this stage, though, a specific example might bring home the point more forcefully than these somewhat crude caricatures of doctrinal difference. To give this I will go back to Müller and compare a brief statement representative of his world certainty, of his outlook on the ultimate nature of existence, with that of Eugene Marais, the South African poet and naturalist who was one of the pioneers of the science of animal behaviour.

First Müller:

How thankful we ought to be every minute of our existence to Him who gives us all richly to enjoy. How little one has deserved this happy life . . . what better, more beautiful, more orderly world could we wish to belong to than that by which we are surrounded and supported on all sides. . . . It is a perfect sin not to be happy in this world.[9]

And now Marais, writing in *The Soul of the White Ant*:

We seek in vain in nature for love, sympathy, pity, justice, altruism, protection of the innocent and weak. From the very beginnings of life we hear a chorus of anguish. Pain is a condition of existence, escape from pain is the purpose of all striving. . . . If nature possesses a universal psyche, it is one far above the common and most impelling feelings of the human psyche. She certainly has never wept in sympathy, nor stretched a hand protectively over even the most beautiful and innocent of her creatures.[10]

Logically, but none the less tragically for that, Marais took his own life in 1936. As Huston Smith has pointed out, the acceptance or rejection of some such concept as God is sometimes, at root, very much a matter of facing life in an attitude of hope rather than despair.[11] For Müller, the face of mother earth bore a warm and welcoming smile, for Marais a snarl of remorseless savagery. For Cipher, informed about a wide range of such opinions, the question is: which one is he to accept?

I have suggested that we are similar in terms of the basic elements of which our lives are composed, and have collectively termed these elements 'the human situation' and located the accuracy of claiming that we *are* in the same house in the fact that whatever shape the individual biography we happen to live through may be, it is lived within the defining constraints of these basic shared conditions. We could, for convenience, symbolize these common elements as the letters of the alphabet. Our difference lies, first, in the particular combination and alignment of these 'letters' which spell out our person, place and history, and, secondly, in the world-view which we accept as providing an accurate overall view of things, i.e. which says something about the alphabet as a whole, or which provides an 'adequate account of the world', to hark back to the passage from Virginia Woolf mentioned in Chapter 1. It is important to emphasize the rather obvious point about our being in the same house lest Cipher's critics think he might disappear down a relativistic bolt-hole, or rather a series of such bolt-holes, such that he 'becomes' Hindu, Buddhist, Christian, Muslim, atheist etc. according to environment rather than assessment, and allows, without further reflection, that there is no problem posed by the existence of such religious variety. 'When in Rome, do as the Romans', is good advice on the level of common-sense, but taken too far it could leave Cipher as a religious chameleon, whose chromatic flexibility would be well-nigh indistinguishable from a situation where no decision had been made about the final colour of things.

This is not to deny the local colour found in every variety of human religiousness. Going back to the alphabet analogy, there are elements of religion addressed to, or expressive of, the specific situations A, AB, ABC, C, CG, GHF, and so on over the immense spectrum of possible letter-combinations in which individuals may find themselves, but there are also elements addressed to, or expressive of, the alphabet itself, which purport to hold good for *any* particular combination of letters, which reach beyond any specific social or cultural environment and address the common elementary aspects of the human situation. As Huston Smith put it, every religion is 'a blend of universal principles and local setting. The former, when lifted out and made clear, speak to man as man, whatever his time or place'.[12] Whilst I would agree with Smith that the local setting aspect is primarily mythological and ritual in nature, his strictures about its inaccessibility to anyone not indigenous to that religion seem somewhat overstated in the light of some recent work in religious studies.

However, this is of little consequence here since our focus will be on *universal principles*. It is when these so called universal principles are involved that the same house/different worlds situation becomes intellectually interesting, if perplexing, and an easy relativistic solution is ruled out. It is when we are dealing with those elements of religion which seem to address *everyone*, regardless of their specific geographical or temporal setting, that the hall of mirrors has the potential to weave a dilemma such as that confronting Cipher. Of course, there may be some difficulty in providing reliable criteria to distinguish between those elements of religion addressed to a universal context and those addressed to, or expressive of, a more local one, but the distinction itself seems valid nonetheless – at least as regards the great world religions. Whether it would hold for some primitive religions is less sure. Certainly, in the passages quoted from Marais and Müller, I think it is clear that they were intended as comments *on the world*, rather than being merely regional ontologies or purely autobiographical statements.

Given, then, that an important part of religion is concerned to provide universal principles by which we may understand and guide our lives in the world, that is, *any* human life in *any* contextual situation, and given also that there is a variety of such principles which are, at least at first sight, incompatible (either we are reborn or we are not; time is either cyclical or linear; the operation of karma and samsara is incompatible with the will of a benificent and all-powerful deity, the self is either eternal or transient), then apart from the questions of why so many different religious pictures of the world appear, that is, different pictures of those elements of the human situation which remain constant amidst all the variations of time and place, and how the different pictures will affect one another as they become more and more inter-conscious, the uncommitted individual such as Cipher is faced with a situation which would seem to demand that he makes some *decision*.

The religiously ambiguous nature of the world which is suggested by a comparison of *sick-souled* and *healthy-minded* outlooks – to apply William James' famous psychological

categories to Marais and Müller[13] – has perhaps been presented most concisely for philosophical discussion by John
Wisdom in his parable of the gardener. Let me quote part of
the original version of this now well-known story, which was
first told by Wisdom to the Aritotelian Society in a paper read
to its members in March 1945:

Two people return to their long neglected garden and find among the
weeds a few of the old plants surprisingly vigorous. One says to the
other 'It must be that a gardener has been coming and doing
something about these plants.' Upon inquiry they find that no
neighbour has ever seen anyone at work in their garden. The first
man says to the other 'He must have worked while people slept.' The
other says 'No, someone would have heard him and besides, any-
body who cared about the plants would have kept down these
weeds.' The first man says 'Look at the way these are arranged.
There is purpose and a feeling for beauty here. I believe that someone
comes, someone invisible to mortal eyes. I believe that the more
carefully we look the more we shall find confirmation of this.' They
examine the garden ever so carefully and sometimes they come on
new things suggesting that a gardener comes and sometimes they
come on new things suggesting the contrary and even that a malici-
ous person has been at work.[14]

Wisdom's parable has had a profound effect on modern
philosophy of religion. For our purposes, though, it is too
simple and also misses out the main character. For neither the
man who believes in the gardener, nor the man who does not
believe in him, has a problem of the same order as that of the
neutral observer standing between them who does not know
which version of events to believe. For believer and unbeliever, respective versions of 'the gardener hypothesis', as
Wisdom terms it, may indeed cease to be experimental, turning out instead to be unshakeable decisions about how to see
the world; but for Cipher, the transition from hypothesis to
conclusion does not come about so easily.

   In *The Adventures of Tristram Shandy*, Laurence Sterne
warns us of precisely those characteristics of hypothesis which
seem to operate in Wisdom's garden. 'It is the nature of a
hypothesis, when once a man has conceived it,' Sterne

remarks, 'that it assimilates everything to itself as proper nourishment; and, from the first moment of your begetting it, it generally grows the stronger by everything you see, hear, read or understand.'[15] The moment a man conceives a hypothesis seems, in the case of Wisdom's garden, to seal his outlook for good. The story seems to be set in a situation where the context of decision is determined by *fate*, not choice, in direct variance, incidentally, to Berger's analysis of the direction in which modernity is taking us.[16] But what of an individual like Cipher who seems to be faced, not with an *a priori* set of personality according to which the world appears theistic or atheistic, so that all its elements are read off accordingly, but rather with a situation of genuine uncertainty where a confusing *variety* of hypotheses jostle for the status of conclusion? For, of course, Cipher is not just faced with a simple choice between two obviously opposing positions, rather he is faced with an apparent multiplicity of hypotheses without any decisive instinctual or fate-dominated impulse towards latching on to any particular one as an unshakeable certainty. He is, moreover, without a clear idea of the inter-relationship between the different hypotheses, or indeed of just how many hypotheses there are.

In the same way as some people believe in God and others do not, Cipher is not sure — and these three positions (to make a theistic simplification of the multiple options in the hall of mirrors) *could* be seen to function as statements of personality, rather than as being constitutive of a situation of perplexity in which evaluation and decision are required. As statements of personality such outlooks would simply serve to announce the different ways in which identical evidence would be drawn into particular interpretative catchment areas. To take a simple example, the theistic believer would then interpret a numinous experience as stemming from some deity, the unbeliever would see it either as illusory or as an aesthetic response to the beauties of nature, and to someone such as Cipher, who stands midway between them, it would appear as an ambiguous experience to which either interpretation *might* apply. So every item of experience would be drawn automatically into one of these broad interpretative streams, whose currents would mould the world in their own *a priori* image as either a theistic, an atheistic or a religiously ambiguous place. This is the sort of situation which we can arrive at when a hypothesis is allowed premature conclusion-status and when the whole religious debate becomes a matter of *who you are*, not *what the world is like*. In such a situation, everyone could settle back to a life of contented fishing by the side of whatever interpretative stream happened to feed their particular psyche, pulling from its waters with reassuring predictability exactly the sort of theological catches they expected. There would be no possibility of drawing something unexpected from the depths, nor of the different streams commingling and causing confusion. In such a world, any religious questions would be settled from the outset, Cipher would feel no *perplexity*. Instead, among a multiplicity of autobiographical comments which related only to specific lives, the need to make a decision would be replaced by the simple act of adding his own signature, and simply signing out of the problem of commitment by saying, in effect, that there is no problem: commitment is decided just by the fact of being; 'I am' already contains 'I believe'.

Again, this is an area of conclusion at which Cipher might, conceivably, arrive, deciding in the end that he must simply *accept* a situation of multiple religious *possibilities* as the hypothesis through which he will see and according to which he will order all that he experiences in the garden of the world. To begin with, though, he will not be content to let matters rest thus. For, while the other denizens of Wisdom's garden might be supposed to have arrived at, or to possess, *satisfactory* outlooks on the world, according at least to their own assessments, Cipher is *not* satisfied with his state of uncertainty and would be loathe to allow it to develop into a conclusion. Unlike Wisdom's characters, for whom religious outlooks are not hypotheses at all, for Cipher they are theories to be tested, mirrors which seem to reflect more than just narcissistic images of the world and, as such, warrant further exploration.

In a potent rewriting of Wisdom's parable, Antony Flew cast down the gauntlet of falsifiability to the believer. To those who accept as certainty the hypothesis that there *is* a gardener, or, in non-metaphorical terms, that God exists, Flew posed the question: 'What would be needed in order for you to *abandon* that belief?' In particular, with reference to the problem of evil — which occurs if the gardener is thought to display the traditional attributes of the Christian God — 'How much suffering and horror would be necessary before a belief in such a God was abandoned?'[17]

From the point of view of some varieties of theistic belief, Flew's question seems unanswerable. But Cipher has already answered it. In seeking to focus on the heart of the matter, in seeking to move to the linchpin of a religious outlook on things, he has accepted that there is some sort of religious experience, some kind of reported encounter with something transcendent, which provides the genesis of any 'positive' variety of the gardener hypothesis and which, if wholly abandoned, would mean that such a hypothesis *could* be seen merely as one possible evaluative vocabulary for a world which is *equally* accurately described by a negative, non-gardener hypothesis (rather than being an account of how things really are, such that alternative outlooks to it are, in fact, mistaken).

Cipher's task at present is to consider religiously positive outlooks on the world, those which assert that 'something is there' which offers peace of mind for his sense of lostness, and to consider them in such a way as to try to reach as near as possible to those moments of experience in which, ultimately, they seem to be rooted, to which the various phenomena expressive of such outlooks refer for their authority, and without which, or so it seems to him, they would wither and die. This, it must be remembered, is an answer to the challenge of falsifiability made from a position of neutrality. Whether or not such a reply would be appropriate, were it to be made from a stance of particular commitment, is not something I can discuss here.

Of course the question which asks: 'What do these moments of vital, originative experience consist of and signify?' will itself be replied to with answers which may flow according to the various hypothetical streams already determined by the predilections of the experiencer, rather than according to any more objective criteria. But unless he self-consciously and deliberately returns to the source, it would be impossible for Cipher to come to a reliable conclusion about which interpretation is most accurate, or to decide if the experience is such that it may indeed bear several interpretations which compete only in terms of congeniality to personality-type, not in terms of what is the case. At this stage in his inquiries, Cipher's focus of interest would seem to be clearly set on trying to share as closely as possible in the experience of the Christian, the Hindu, the Buddhist and so on, so that he may arrive at a perspective in which he may try to judge for himself the nature of their vision of the world. In terms of Wisdom's parable, he needs to see the garden through their eyes before deciding what can, in fact, be seen there.

Given the situation of religious diversity which Cipher needs to explore in moving towards some decision about commitment in the context of a religiously plural world, the situation of different accounts suggesting worlds as radically different as that of Müller and Marais for the same house (or garden, if you prefer Wisdom), *how* is he to proceed with his investigation?

Religious studies, which has been at least partially responsible for bringing to our notice the immense variety of religious worlds inhabited by humankind and the extent to which they appear to differ – and which, as we have seen, has been *largely* responsible for facilitating Cipher's perspective on the hall of mirrors – has, increasingly, become concerned to provide an appropriate methodological vehicle for investigative inter-global travel between the different worlds of religious meaning. So, at this point, Cipher may again turn his attention to the disciplinary area which has fathered his dilemma. This time he will focus his attention on that one particular strand, from the complex and confusing web which surrounds this whole area, which views the so-called 'phenomenology of religion' as a methodological vehicle by which the different religious worlds may be explored in depth.

To use John S. Dunne's phrase, phenomenology of religion

so conceived provides a means of effectively '*passing over*'[18] into the religious situation which one wants to investigate and 'coming back' with a clearer understanding of it. It is a means of passing over to someone else's religious world of meaning so that we may try to see how things appear when viewed through that perspective. It is an attempt to place us, so far as this is possible, in the other person's shoes, so that we might stand there and walk with him, observing and feeling what occurs, with a closeness which would be impossible for an 'external' study, where we stood rooted to the spot and made no attempt at passing over beyond the mere turning of an already judgemental gaze in the direction of the phenomena concerned (such as seems to be the perspective adopted by the denizens of Wisdom's garden).

Phenomenology of religion viewed as such seeks to offer to its sufficiently competent practitioner as non-secondhand an insight as it is possible to achieve into what animates the different vitalities and movements of meaning within any particular religious outlook. Its basic motivating idea is quite straightforward: to try to apprehend someone else's religion *as it appears to them*, rather than focusing attention on how it appears to us from a non-phenomenological standpoint. To achieve this perspective it is necessary to maintain a deliberate open-mindedness, which postpones making any value judgements, and to let oneself be moved, if only temporarily, by the same currents of meaning as stir the believer under study. Such a method thus relies to a great extent on the disciplined use of the imagination and is focused more on individual religiousness than on religions considered as separate theoretical entities.

Winston L. King offers a clear statement of the goal of phenomenology of religion viewed in these terms. It is, he says, 'to observe all types of religiousness from the veritable inside, and yet escape to tell all to outsiders – including one's own outside, ordinary self'.[19] Ninian Smart takes us a little further, pointing out that this sort of approach refers to

the procedure of getting at the meaning of a religious act or symbol or institution *for the participants*. It refers, in other words, to a kind of imaginative participation in the world of the actor.[20]

Passing over thus rejects any picture of observer and observed facing each other across the interface of method. Here method becomes more like an encircling hoop which seeks to bind them close together for the duration of any period of inquiry. Gerardus van der Leeuw, considered by many to be one of the key figures in the phenomenological tradition within religious studies, provides a further pointer towards what may be involved in this type of exercise. According to his analysis, phenomenology of religion necessitates 'not only the description of what is visible from the outside, but above all the experience born of what can only become reality after it has been admitted into the life of the observer himself'.[21] In other words, the phenomenological observer is not to be seen as a white-coated diagnostician standing by the patient and noting every symptom – although *part* of his work *will* involve such meticulous observation. Rather, he seeks to move close enough to the subject of study so that the religious pulse makes itself felt against, or even within, his own skin.

The current of thought which advocates such deliberate and disciplined use of our imagination in the attempt to understand religion, extends beyond those who actually talk about phenomenology or term themselves phenomenologists. Rudolf Otto, for example, called for 'penetrative imaginative sympathy with what passes in the other person's mind',[22] and proceeded in *The Idea of the Holy* with what some have seen as a phenomenological exercise.[23] Before Otto, James Haughton Woods suggested that the key task in the study of religion is 'to reproduce, as if real to us, all the ideas which compose the mental picture present to the stranger, to repeat in our own imagination all the feelings or will-attitudes which are bound up with this experience'.[24] More recently, Wilfred Cantwell Smith has cautiously suggested that by the exercise of 'imaginative sympathy',[25] cross-checked by various other methods, it may be possible to 'infer what goes on in another's mind and heart'.[26]

In employing this type of method – which can be referred to as 'passing over' so as to avoid the various unwanted philosophical connotations which 'phenomenology of religion' might suggest – Cipher will attempt to put into practice the old Red-Indian proverb which insists that we ought not to judge a man until we have walked a mile in his mocassins. Or, to take another elucidating parallel, in a sense he will be applying to the images in the hall of mirrors Father Brown's strategy for dealing with serious crimes – for when G. K. Chesterton's famous detective is asked the secret of his success in solving apparently insoluble cases of murder, he replies: 'The secret is . . . it was I who killed all those people.'[27] This is not, of course, a literal confession of multiple homicide, nor does it mean that he embarks on anything as simple as a 'psychological reconstruction', but rather, as he puts it: 'I really did see myself, and my real self, committing the murders. . . . I mean that I thought and thought about how a man might come to be like that until I realized that I really *was* like that, in everything except actual final consent to the action.'[28] Such a technique was, he adds, once suggested to him by a friend as a sort of religious exercise.[29] It is a religious exercise in which he comes to share a murderer's outlook with an intimacy which some might find fearful or distasteful, for he continues the process: 'till I have bent myself into the posture of his hunched and peering hatred; till I see the world with his bloodshot and squinting eyes, looking between the blinkers of his half-willed concentration; looking up the short and sharp perspective of a strangled road to a pool of blood. Till I am really a murderer.'[30] Or, to take a third parallel, in adopting passing over, Cipher will be utilizing an expanded version of what William Golding calls 'kinaesthesia',[31] a sympathetic identification with someone else's movement – a technique which, incidentally, Golding develops to superb effect in offering a 'passing over' to prehistoric religiousness in his novel *The Inheritors*.

Cipher will employ passing over, in the hope that it will take him to a perspective from which he may view, more closely and directly than would otherwise be possible, those points of originative and confirming experience from which, in an important sense, the images in the hall of mirrors stem, and on which they rely for their status as legitimate bearers of peace of mind. He will, in short, use passing over to take him to – or at least *towards* – the heart of the matter.

This method is based on the assumption, perhaps voiced more often by writers and poets than by those who study religion, that no human outlook can be so alien to us that we cannot come to understand it. Such an assumption finds marvellous expression, to take just one example, in Walt Whitman's 'Song of Myself', where the poet acknowledges, across a wide range of religious and historical settings, what he terms 'duplicates of myself' under all the 'scrape-lipped and pipe-legged concealments'.[32] This assumption of accessibility is, of course, based on the belief that we all occupy the *same house*, however different our perception of the world may be.

Whether or not the process of passing over will be *successful* in leading him through religious arterial systems to the source of their pulse, is not something to be decided without a careful attempt to apply its principles, and this is not something which can be attempted here, although some possible *consequences* of success will be considered in the next chapter. Thus, to some extent, a consideration of the possible objections which might be cast in the way of passing over is better postponed until we have seen it in action. There is one objection, though, which it is, perhaps, best to mention very briefly at this stage since, if accepted, it would simply deny the possibility of the whole endeavour.

This objection, the quaintly named 'if I were a horse fallacy' has been put forward by the anthropologist E. E. Evans-Pritchard in his *Theories of Primitive Religion*.[33] The objection, as its name implies, refers to and condemns immoderate notions of how far empathy − i.e. entering into another's personality and imaginatively re-experiencing his experiences − can actually extend. Few of us would seriously wish to claim that we could come to know what it felt like to be a horse. But is it any less ridiculous to claim that we know how it feels to occupy some distant world of religious meaning which is not our own, such as, for example, that of a Buddhist or a devotee of the Hindu goddess Kali?

Accusations of committing the 'if I were a horse fallacy' are generally accompanied by the idea that the open-mindedness necessary for passing over in the first place, that is, the ability not to let our own point of view obscure the outlook we wish to examine – cannot in fact be sustained beyond a fairly limited level, even in cases where the absurdity of such a venture is not so patently obvious as it would be if it were turned in an equine direction.

I would suggest, quite simply, that commonsense and a study of the actual imaginative outreach displayed in works of literature could successfully refute any argument which sought to show that imaginative re-experiencing, of the sort demanded by passing over, is simply not possible. The question of the *degree* to which it is possible remains open to research, as does the question of the extent to which it would be useful to Cipher. Obviously we would do well to eschew any thoughts of being able to perform fantastical feats of imaginative accuracy, such as, for example, coming to know *exactly* what it felt like to enter a prehistoric cave sanctuary, to understand precisely all the nuances of meaning attached to the various rituals performed there, and to grasp the way in which the numinous was experienced and expressed at the very dawn of human religiousness. It would, however, be just as foolish – if not in quite so spectacular a fashion – to underrate the flexibility and accuracy of the informed and disciplined imagination. It is enough that passing over takes us closer *towards* the heart of some particular type of religiousness than we might otherwise have approached. We do not have to insist that such a process is one hundred per cent successful before we can advocate it as a method by which Cipher may proceed.

Let us, finally, try to anticipate what the result might be if Cipher embarked on a policy of passing over in the attempt to resolve his situation of informed neutrality. Maybe we can find a clue here by building on Ninian Smart's analogy and comparing the practitioner of such a discipline to the actor.[34] As Mircea Eliade has remarked, through the voice of Bibiscescu, one of the characters in his novel *The Forbidden Forest*, the actor

identifies himself in turn with innumerable human existences, and he suffers, if he is a good actor, just as the character he represents on stage suffers in his life. This means that he knows in a single life-time the passions, the hopes, the suffering and the revelation of fifty or a hundred lives.[35]

Whether the extensive repertoire of religious roles which passing over would result in would, in fact, help Cipher towards a clear sense of his *own* identity and purpose, or if it would act simply to confuse and perplex him yet further, will, of course, depend on what actually lies at the heart of the matter and the extent to which it can be reached.

5

A Return to Beginnings

Faced with the many different worlds of religious meaning which the various facets of the hall of mirrors seem to reflect on to his existence, each offering an account of it which, if accepted, would effectively counter his feelings of insignificance, mystery and meaninglessness – his sense of being lost – it was suggested in the last chapter that Cipher should embark on a strategy of 'passing over'. That is, he should attempt to investigate the reflections which perplex him in such a way as to share as closely as possible the outlook on the world of those whose faith constitutes the reflections in the first place. In particular, Cipher wants to be brought closer to the experiential roots which seem to underlie such outlooks, so that he may come to see for himself how these are perceived by those who take them to be sufficiently authoritative to give meaning to the complex religious structures stemming from them, and to warrant their own commitment being expressed in terms of (and indeed adding to) the various resources afforded by these structures. Cipher is not interested in the straightforward accumulation of information *about* religious outlooks on the world. As we saw in Chapter 2, the information to which he already has access constitutes a potential barrier to his arriving at any conclusions about commitment. Rather, he is interested in arriving at a perspective from which he may judge whether or not any particular image in the hall of mirrors is a legitimate source of peace of mind.

His focus of attention will be set more on the individual Hindu or Christian or Buddhist, who has apparently *found* peace of mind through his faith, than on 'Hinduism', 'Christianity' or 'Buddhism' considered as impersonal, historical entities – although obviously the two areas overlap. He is concerned to share the apparently sense-giving perspectives on the world offered by the different varieties of religiousness, and to locate within these perspectives the experience of whatever transcendent state or entity it is which, ultimately, seems to give them life and to allow that they be accepted as veridical by those who look through them at the world, and guide their lives accordingly.

It has been suggested that passing over could be likened to the teaching of the Indian proverb which suggests that we do not judge a man until we have walked a mile in his mocassins. In walking that mile Cipher will not wander aimlessly in circles, as if on some sort of spiritual sight-seeing trip around the new religious realm to which passing over gives access. Rather, his steps will be directed resolutely towards what he takes to be the heart of the matter, the perception of which may allow him to resolve his dilemma.

According to the French diarist Amiel, the presence of whose journal on Cipher's bookshelves we have already noted, the same process is required to understand a drama, an existence, a biography or an individual. That process, says Amiel,

is a putting back of the bird into the egg,
of the plant into its seed, a reconstruction
of the whole genesis of the being in question.

Amiel's remarks on understanding drama are useful in reminding us of the parallel which may be drawn between 'passing over' and acting and for suggesting the extent to which this sort of endeavour may involve *a return to beginnings*.

The *need* to return to beginnings, to somehow start again, to discover the source, the origin, to get back to some simple, initial level where there is no confusion, doubt or falsehood, at which we may remain in – or from which we may progress to – a state of being which is clear, authentic, true – which satisfies us in some way that our existence before such a return failed to do – is, I would argue, a common human impulse.

Such a need can find expression on a variety of planes.

Indeed it would make an interesting study to trace the different forms in which it has appeared in the course of history. On the intellectual level, for example, Descartes determined to rid himself of all the uncertain opinions and beliefs he had formerly held and then to start out again from a new beginning, from a foundation of incorrigible knowledge. While, on a more tangible level, Henry David Thoreau shed the conventional material luxuries and burdens of human society and went to live in a simple wooden hut which he had built himself in the woods at Walden, this return to simplicity being undertaken because he wished to start again, concerning himself this time only with the fundamental essentials of life as he thought they occurred close to nature. Combining both physical and mental aspects of this need for renewal, for a return to (or a discovery of) some absolutely real and essential source, some fundamental ground, is the Hindu figure of the *sannyasin* who divests himself of all material goods and then, hopefully aided by this practical parallel, engages in rigorous meditative exercises in an attempt to throw off all the superficial layers of personality so as, eventually, to arrive at the absolute beginning of things, the real self, the *Atman*. Doubtless parallels to such an endeavour could be found in most religions, perhaps especially in their monastic forms; for the need to return to beginnings, to be in some sense 'born again', often finds expression in an overtly religious setting.

Of course, this type of simplifying procedure which seeks to cut through unwanted accretions and find some point of beginning on which to found a new way of thinking or living, suggests a prior state of dissatisfaction, confusion or complexity. With Descartes it was the realization that his whole structure of knowledge was susceptible to radical doubt; with Thoreau it was a disenchantment with the concerns of ordinary mundane life in a middle-class urban setting, a conviction that such concerns are peripheral, of only superficial value; with the *sannyasin* it is the belief that this material world and our empirical selves are of only secondary reality.

The state of dissatisfaction, confusion and complexity which prompts Cipher towards the return to beginnings offered by the process of passing over, is constituted by his

awareness of the different worlds of religious meaning con-
tained in the hall of mirrors. Cipher is *dissatisfied* because his
uncommitted stance does not provide an adequate response to
his feelings of insignificance, mystery and meaninglessness.
This does not mean that he is assuming *a priori* that such
feelings may be satisfactorily countered by some view of
things so that his life will become significant, meaningful, and
with any mystery in it safely curbed to that of a positive
wondering variety, rather than its more unnerving sibling. It
may well be that there is simply no peace of mind to be found,
in the sense of locating a positive reassuring response to his
sense of lostness. Moreover, as we noted earlier, 'peace of
mind' may be something of a misnomer for the various world
certainties offered by the religions. But as things stand, with
Cipher informed about a wide range of *possible* sense-giving
commitments, his attitude of neutrality towards them, of
neither acceptance or rejection but simply informedness about
them, is unsatisfactory, given the fact that among them may
be precisely what he is looking for. He is *confused* by the
number of possibilities to which he *might* commit himself,
and, furthermore, uncertain of their inter-relationship. It is
not, as we have seen, just a matter of deciding between a set of
clearly numbered options (though this in itself would not be
exactly easy) but also of deciding how many options there are,
where the boundaries between them fall, and where any areas
of overlap occur. Lastly, Cipher feels the situation is too
complex, because of the glut of information which, as a child
of the third age of religious studies, he has at his disposal and
which has enabled him to see the hall of mirrors from the
perspective he does.

Dissatisfaction, confusion, complexity – Cipher's situation
has exactly the characteristics which we might expect would
impel him towards a new beginning, which would suggest a
return to or an establishing of some simpler state: and in fact
Cipher *has* already started to simplify things, his return
towards beginnings has begun. Thus having noted the potential of information to act as an inimical force, we have seen
how he can adopt various commonsense strategies to cut the
problem down to size. Within that reduced area he has,

moreover, identified a precise target, namely the experiential linchpin, the heart of the matter, the salamander, which all the various aspects of the religious images in some way express and to which they eventually refer back in asserting their sense and value. Finally, in passing over, he has located a methodological vehicle which may take him accurately towards this target rather than misdirecting his attention to some refracted image of it, as it is seen through some external explanatory medium which makes no real effort to see things from the point of view of the believer.

As Edward Said has remarked:

Without at least a sense of beginning, nothing can really be done, much less ended. This is as true for the literary critic as it is for the philosopher, the scientist, or the novelist [or, we might add, for the individual in the hall of mirrors] . . . the more crowded or confused a field appears the more a beginning, fictional or not, seems *imperative*.[2]

In the crowded and confused setting of the hall of mirrors, Cipher has already felt – and started to act upon – the force of this imperative. This chapter will concentrate on explaining exactly how 'passing over' may be seen as a response to it, as a beginnings orientated activity, and on anticipating something of what might happen when Cipher actually applies this method and moves towards the point or points of genesis at which it is aimed.

In what sense, then, is passing over an attempt to return to beginnings? The question can be answered by comparing Cipher's quest to the famous passage in the Chandogya Upanishad where Uddalaka is teaching his son Svetaketu by employing a series of analogies. At one point Svetaketu is told to bring a fruit from the banyan tree and to split it in two. He does so and is asked what he sees. 'These extremely fine seeds,' he replies. He is then told to split the seeds, and again asked what is there. 'Nothing at all,' is his reply.[3] Leaving aside the metaphysical moral which Upanishadic thinking draws from the story, we might see Svetaketu as being engaged in a search for a point of beginning from which stems the complex structure of the fully grown tree. In a somewhat similar progression, faced with the many-branched and densely foliaged tree of religion, Cipher is seeking to find some generative thread or core which enlivens and gives rise to the whole structure.

He is *not* engaged in trying to seek out some sort of single point of *historical* origin somewhere at the dawn of human consciousness which would explain the genesis of all subsequent religious phenomena, just as Svetaketu is not looking for some point of vegetative genesis in prehistory which might be seen as the cause of all subsequent plant life. Nor is he engaged in reduction, in the sense of trying to dismantle religion so as to arrive at some fundamental element which might be elevated to a point of absolute importance, with everything else brushed aside as irrelevant, just as it would be similarly misguided to take the seed as qualifying the rest of the tree as somehow unnecessary. Rather, through passing over, Cipher hopes to be placed in a position of sufficient closeness to that of the believer or believers under study, that he can feel how every element of their particular religiousness is live and significant, how it leads back to and stems from an arterial system or seedbed which gives it life and without which it would lose much of its reason for existing.

Unlike Svetaketu, however, who approaches things from an external perspective, who plucks something from the tree and proceeds to dissect it in isolation in order to arrive at some sort of originative point, Cipher's approach will be more holistic. Accepting serious expressions of religiousness as integrated organic wholes whose vitality – and viability – is best gauged when they are taken as such, rather than when they are subjected to investigative dismemberment, Cipher will attempt to return to beginnings, not by lopping off some likely looking point of genesis and saying: 'this is the starting point', but by feeling how such a starting point reaches out its influence even to the extremities of a religious structure. From such immediately visible extremities, he will attempt to work his way back towards the source.

It is no use trying to get back to the heart of the matter, if

you have made a series of methodological cuts which effectively leave you with several neatly labelled piles, one of
leaves, one of branches, one of bark, and so on. The temptation is, of course, to say that whilst Svetaketu studies trees *in
vitro*, Cipher would seek to study them *in vivo*, but at this
point the 'if I were a horse fallacy' mentioned in the last
chapter might deliver a resounding – and perhaps well
deserved – kick, if only to remind us of the danger which
mixing or overloading metaphors may pose to the
methodological credibility of passing over. The sense of
beginnings which Cipher has is one which, from the point of
view of informed neutrality, respects the religious person as
providing the context in which is located the starting point
relevant to deciding whether or not to accept some particular
type of religiousness as genuinely offering peace of mind. As
we shall shortly discover, Cipher, like Svetaketu, will, in fact,
be left with a similarly intangible heart of the matter to that
which is visible within the innermost kernel of the banyan
tree's seeds.

At this stage it is helpful in understanding more fully the
nature of Cipher's intended investigative course of action, to
turn once again to religious studies and see where he stands in
relation to it. It might well be supposed that, given his
beginnings-orientated approach, any relationship must now
be a straightforward one of simple ostracism. At this point,
perhaps more clearly than at any other, we can see how unlike
are Cipher's quest and *some* conceptions of the academic
study of religion. For in focusing on religious experience, in
seeking to draw close to the originating source, the pulse, the
heart of the matter, the salamander – however the transcendent element in religion may be labelled – Cipher will be very
obviously breaking those strictures marking out its area of
interest, which are applied in some understandings of the
discipline which is variously named comparative religion,
science of religion, history of religions, phenomenology of
religion and so on – what I am referring to collectively as
religious studies and have identified as the disciplinary area
which has been largely responsible for making possible
Cipher's perplexing plural perspective, i.e. for fostering his
awareness of the hall of mirrors.

Georg Schmid, for example, has noted how a substantial part of religious studies takes as the only legitimate object of study something which is completely secondary for religion. Thus he writes:

Of secondary interest for religion is its own thanksgiving, hope, prayer, sensitivity, teaching and behaviour as well as all the material in which this religious experience expresses itself. These are interesting for religion only in their relation to the reality to which all religious experience refers. . . . Modern (religious studies) limits itself on principle to religious data not as referring beyond but as interesting in themselves. Instead of letting itself be directed by the data to the reality beyond the data, it becomes intensely interested in the director and the act of directing.[4]

Cipher, on the other hand, is interested precisely in that supposed reality to which religious data refer and from which they stem. He is concerned to get to the heart (or hearts) of the matter, rather than remaining mesmerized by the complex corporate bodies which it (or they) animate, and which seem to constitute the area staked out by *some* scholars as the territory of religious studies, within which it may bring to bear the full range of its methodological sophistication, but beyond which it must not go on pain of academic excommunication. Cipher is interested in what is pointed at, not the finger which is pointing. Thus whilst what we might dub 'territorial' religious studies may focus on and be fascinated by all the ritual details of prayer or worship, Cipher will be interested in seeing more closely that to which such religious activities are directed, and which, ultimately, gives them sense in terms of their being aspects of a legitimate peace-of-mind-offering outlook. Only by focusing on the experiential *beginnings* of religion, the salamander rather than the slap, to reiterate the central metaphor of Chapter 3, can he hope to arrive at a standpoint from which he may make a satisfactory decision about commitment. For so far as Cipher can see, serious religiousness derives and rests its weight on such experience and holds whatever validity it can finally claim precisely by reference to this elusive locus. The only reason he should, in the end, accept an image from the hall of mirrors as compellingly authoritative, as opposed to being attractive or pragmatically acceptable, would seem to be if he too could come to endorse the potency of these originative points. Thus, inevitably, his endeavour will be at odds with a substantial body of academic opinion. Not that this should come as any great surprise: for as we have noted already, Cipher is not attempting to write some sort of single-handed natural history of religion, but, rather, to reach a point of personal world decision.

Not all scholars fall within that group which characterizes the subject in such a way that what religious experience refers to is ruled strictly off-limits. So it would be misleading to suppose that Cipher is now so entirely cut adrift from his fathering discipline that he could not hope to find any points of elucidating contact with it. On the contrary, there are many scholars who, at times, seem to be walking in a more or less similar direction to the one in which he is seeking to go.

In his translation of the Upanishads, for example, Gordon Milburn writes that the whole aim of his work is:

to enable my readers personally to feel something of the inspiration which moved the original writers so that their reading may become . . . a reproduction of the devotional contemplation of supreme reality in which this literature took its origin.[5]

For Milburn, then, a reading of the Upanishads is of primary concern not for any historical or linguistic points which it might raise about the writing of this type of sacred text, but because through such a reading we may somehow be brought into close proximity with that experience from which they derive. As such, Milburn accepts that as translator he must sacrifice exegesis for what he calls the transmission of inspiration.

Likewise Lewis and Slater write of the Vedic hymns which preceded the Upanishads:

Some of the earliest hymns have a poetic beauty and numinous quality, even in transcription, which awakens in us, as they presumably stirred in their composers and original reciters, a reaction similar to the experience of God made possible for us normally by other means today.[6]

In short, for them the slap still has a mnemonic potency which has remained unbroken either by translation or some three and a half thousand years of history, so that it still provides an effective reminder of the salamander which presumably called it into existence in the first place. In view of such findings, it seems clear that at least some religious phenomena appear to point insistently beyond themselves, so that a focus which demanded that we confine our attention to them, rather than what they refer to, would be a somewhat artificial, if not dishonest, constriction. (Unfortunately, Lewis and Slater do not go into details of what they refer to, with such intriguing commonplaceness, as the normal present-day means of experiencing God. Clearly if such means do exist they would be of intense interest to Cipher!)

Along the same lines as Milburn and Lewis & Slater, we find in Rudolf Otto's seminal study *The Idea of the Holy* some similar ideas about the possibility of focusing attention on the experiential beginnings of religiousness. Of the numinous, the originative sense of the holy whose presence, he claims, lies at the innermost core of all religion, Otto writes, 'It will be our endeavour to suggest this unnamed something to the reader so far as we may, so that he may himself feel it'.[7] He is somewhat dubious of the power of words alone to do this, hence his call – noted in the last chapter – for 'penetrative imaginative sympathy.' Raimundo Panikkar sums up well the nature – and the value – of the sort of starting point which Otto seems to reach in *The Idea of the Holy*, which is arguably the most influential return to beginnings in modern religious thought, when he notes that 'a nonconceptual awareness allows different translations of the same transconceptual reality for different notation systems'.[8] Thus Otto notes a common element underlying Isaiah, Chapter 6, and the eleventh chapter of the *Bhagavad Gita*,[9] and he can quite confidently assert that 'Allah is mere "numen" and is in fact precisely Yahweh in his pre-Mosaic form and upon a larger scale'.[10] In reaching some sort of pre-conceptual or pre-verbal point of genesis, and in suggesting that it is possible to evoke and awaken such a sense of vital beginning and sustenance in the minds of his readers, Otto clearly points in the direction in which Cipher seeks to go. He seems also to suggest, incidentally, that by a return to such a beginning we may pass below the turbulence of religions as they are perceived in all their discordant diversity by a first glance around the hall of mirrors, and find important areas of continuity underlying them.

Although he does not voice Otto's desire to take his readers towards such a point of religious beginning, it is interesting to see in R. C. Zaehner's *Hinduism*, which remains one of the best single volume introductions to this area of religiousness, that the author himself is sensitive to the religious power of the symbols he studies, not just to their historical or mythological significance. Thus, for example, he does not simply offer us an historical analysis of the deity Shiva from his earliest primitive form in the Indus Valley civilization, through his Vedic manifestation as Rudra, to his place as one of the three high gods of Hinduism. Rather, he comments on 'the great God Rudra-Shiva, the most numinous and disturbing, representation of deity that Hinduism was to produce'.[11] That is, as something whose power he can apparently feel and evaluate himself.

Studying an act of prayer or worship in depth, may, Jacques Waardenburg notes with some surprise, give us a glimpse of the 'intended object' of the person praying or worshipping; it may reveal something of the reality which they assume they are addressing through whatever ritual forms they use.[12] Catching sight of this reality is the explicit aim of David R. Kinsley's brilliant study of the Hindu deities Kali and Krishna. Indeed he presents his book *The Sword and the Flute* as a deliberate attempt to 'understand Krishna and Kali by trying to glimpse Kali's sword and hear Krishna's flute'.[13] In other words, he is attempting to see the vital originative force which, according to Hindus, underlies Hindu spirituality, and is symbolized by devotees of Kali and Krishna in terms of a sword or a flute, according to whether its manifestation is perceived as malevolent or benign (this to make a simple bi-polar duality of what is, in fact, taken to be single and continuous). Kinsley is less interested in amassing historical or mythological data than in, as he puts it, discerning in the presences of these two beings 'hints of the transcendentally real',[14] as it has been perceived in Hinduism; and certainly, in his hands, we do sometimes seem to travel smoothly and easily towards the heart of an 'alien' religious world. Of Kali, perhaps to Western eyes the most immediately distasteful goddess in the Hindu pantheon, since she is usually portrayed as demonic and bloodthirsty in the most lurid detail, Kinsley writes:

Meditation on Kali, confrontation with her, even the slightest glimpse of her, restores man's hearing, thus enabling or forcing a keener perception of things around him. Confronted with the vision of Kali he begins to hear, perhaps for the first time, those sounds he has so carefully censored in the illusion of his physical immortality. . . . He may also be able to hear, with his keener perception, the howl of laughter that mocks his pretence, the mad laugh of Kali, the mistress of time, to whom he will succumb inevitably despite his deafness or cleverness. . . . She invites man to join in her mad dance in the cremation ground, she invites him to make of himself a cremation ground so that she may dance there, releasing him from the fetters of a bound existence. She invites man to approach the cremation ground without fear, thus releasing him to participate in his true destiny, which lies beyond this whirlygig of samsara in transcendent release.[15]

This is quite a series of invitations, and the question of where, precisely, Kinsley stands in relation to the purported transcendent reality of which Kali is a symbol, in order to have received them so clearly, is insistently posed. In this sort of work we do indeed seem sometimes to catch a glimpse of something bright and enticing – but is it Kali's sword or a religious version of Macbeth's dagger? Are we brought face to face with – or unnervingly close to – some transcendent element of Hindu religiousness, or are we only encountering a creation of the 'heat oppressed brain' which has reached some sort of unhealthy spiritual boiling point through too much 'passing over'?

In Chapter 2 we referred to a passage from Cipher's journal where he likened his awareness of many religious outlooks on the world to being blinded by many different lights. To continue *that* metaphor, passing over is an attempt to return to beginnings in the sense of trying to move from the outer-most, immediately visible reaches of a particular beam, ever inwards towards its source. And, as we have seen, some work within religious studies seems also to move in this direction, with results which would suggest that Cipher is not envisaging attempting the impossible. Indeed, given the number of scho-lars who seem to advocate some form of 'passing over', with all the implications which such a methodology has, it is perhaps rather strange that some work apparently moves in the *opposite* direction, erecting some sort of crash barrier beyond which, apparently, we must not go. Thus, putting it with reference to a study of Islam, W. Brede Kristensen writes:

We cannot become [Muslims] when we try to understand Islam, if we could, our study would be at an end: we should ourselves then directly experience the reality.[16]

Leaving aside the apparent implication that Muslims cannot study their own faith, how could such an assertion be so confidently made, unless Kristensen himself had directly experienced this reality and concluded that the *only* response to it was an Islamic one, rather than, say, a Hindu or a Buddhist one? (In which case, had such a direct experience occurred, he would, of course, by his own criteria *be* a Muslim.) His remark *assumes* that a study of Islam has to do with an underlying reality which is exclusively Islamic. But many who have studied faiths other than their own have found that coming close to the transcendent reality, appar-ently perceived within an 'alien' tradition, in fact positively enriches their *own* religiousness, rather than encouraging some sort of apostasy. Yet how could this be, if the matter were as cut and dried as Kristensen suggests?[17] His mapping of the relationship between believer and observer, and the implied relationship between varieties of religiousness, is surely misleading simplistic.

Many – and Kristensen would surely be counted among them – seem to take the view of Edward Farley that the actual reality-apprehendings of a determinate community (of faith) do not occur in the uncovering analyses of phenomenology, but in *participating* in the community itself.[18]

This may well hold for phenomenology in its guise of objective descriptive study, but 'passing over', we must remember, is not simply another name for this sort of approach. If we take seriously calls for 'penetrative imaginative sympathy' to see into the hearts and minds of the believers,[19] then it would surely be reasonable to put passing over as close to *participation* as it is to *observation*. Indeed the roles of participator and observer in terms of two quite separate non-overlapping functions, can only hold within an investigative situation where religious studies conforms to what Schmid saw as a focusing on what is of secondary importance for religion itself. The line between the two roles tends to blur when we see how scholars like Kinsley, Otto and Milburn apparently experience, or come very close to experiencing, the same reality as the believers.

In his study of emptiness ('sunyata') in the thought of the second century Buddhist philosopher Nagarjuna, Frederick J. Streng comments:

The aim to 'understand', as it is conceived in this study, must be differentiated from the Buddhist disciple's aim to know the truth of 'emptiness'. While both the Buddhist disciple and the historian of religions express a desire to know the meaning of 'emptiness', the disciple wants to realize this personally within himself and would find the historical and phenomenological distinctions that we will make here a diversion from his goal.[20]

The trouble is, exactly as it was in Wisdom's garden, Cipher is an uneasy middle-man caught between two less problematic positions. In Streng's study, historian of religions and Buddhist disciple are given clearly demarcated roles. What, though, of the individual like Cipher, who has been informed of one by the other and is uncertain where to stand in relation to that information? What of someone for whom the history of religions has provided access to a variety of points of apparent contact with transcendent reality?

The question of whether or not passing over will be *successful* in returning Cipher to the starting points he seeks is, I think, best postponed until he has actually attempted to put its methodology into practice. However, even if his passing over does *not* take him to a perspective from which he may directly observe or experience the transcendent realities which seem to animate the various forms of religiousness which interest him, his endeavours will, presumably (unless he is utterly incompetent), take him *towards* such realities, so that, at the very least, he will be told about such points of beginning by those who feel that they do stand *directly* in their light. The problem is, such eye-witness accounts seem to have some rather special characteristics which might make us wonder if they would be of much use in helping Cipher to reach some decision about commitment. The special characteristic on which I wish to focus in particular is that of *ineffability*, the apparent inexpressibility of religious experience, such that some have claimed it occurs wholly beyond words.

Of course many things *are* said about religion, even about (indeed especially about) what appear to be its most descriptively elusive originative elements. Thus there is much 'talk' of one sort or another about, for example, Brahman, God, Nirvana, Tao and so on. Indeed, whole religious structures might, perhaps, be viewed as efforts across a wide range of mediums – linguistic, behavioural, artistic, musical and so on – to express the nature and significance of these starting points (which are, of course, often seen as destinations too). But, sooner or later, in all such expressive instances we come to a core of ineffability which denies any of them final sanction as being adequately expressive, and which generates yet more attempts at expression. The salamander, the originative reality, gives rise to an extensive outgrowth of tangible phenomena, at the heart of which it remains behind a mysterious opaqueness ringed with silence.

The mystic gives clearest voice to this inner core of ineffability, and it is in his particular type of discourse that the live wire of originative experience which seems to run throughout the religious realm, appears closest to the surface. In the examples which follow, then, I am taking the view that what has been so strikingly described by the mystic is, as Winston King put it, 'legitimately and necessarily present in more pedestrian varieties and positive forms of religious expression',[21] even if we may have to look more closely to see it; that mysticism is, in Paul van Buren's words, 'an extreme form of what is genuine in religion',[22] rather than being some sort of idiosyncratic or deviant offshoot from it. In mysticism we can see more immediately that beginning towards which a passing over into almost any form of religiousness would seem eventually to take us.

A passage from Eckhart perhaps most clearly identifies the radical unlikeness, the complete non-comparability, which seems to characterize the ineffable starting point of religion. He writes:

All words fail . . . nothing true can be spoken of God . . . no one can express what he actually is. We can say nothing of God *because nothing is like him*.[23]

This denial of all possible comparisons, the claimed ineffectiveness of likeness in this area of experience, is a common feature found in accounts of religious beginnings. The passage from Eckhart is, for example, clearly reminiscent of the rhetorical query posed in Isaiah, 40.18, 'To whom then will you liken God or to what likeness compare with him?' And when Muhammad was asked about the distinguishing attributes of the God he spoke of, the answer he gave (rather, the answer which, according to Islamic belief, was revealed to him) was:

Say, God is one God; the eternal; he begetteth not, neither is he begotten and there is not anyone like unto him.[24]

But for sheer thoroughness in excluding all possible forms of comparison, the account of Brahman given by Shankara (who is sometimes dubbed the Thomas Aquinas of Hinduism) is, I think, unparalleled:

There is no class of substance to which the Brahman belongs, no common genus. It cannot therefore be denoted by words which like 'being' in the ordinary sense signify a category of things. Nor can it be denoted by quality for it is without qualities; nor yet by activity, because it is without activity. ... neither can it be denoted by relationship for it is without a second. Therefore it cannot be defined by word or idea, as the scripture says, it is the one before whom words recoil.[25]

Whereas Cipher *begins* his quest threatened by the sheer bulk of information about religion, it seems as if passing over, his attempt to return to beginnings, may — ironically — simply act to invert the problem. Where once information seemed to be an inimical force, it now seems that a complete *lack* of information may prevent him from making a world decision. For how is he to reach some sort of decision about religious commitment, if nothing can be said about the nature of the experiences which seem to underlie and validate its different varieties?

Assuming that Cipher *will* be led towards an encounter with what is taken by many to be the transcendent, though whether at first or second hand we leave open to research, and assuming that such a starting point exhibits the sort of ineffability found in mystical literature, then three areas of consequence for his quest are, perhaps, worth indicating.

First: It is fascinating to speculate about how Cipher might conceptualize and describe some starting point of transcendent reality, for in a sense he is religiously multilingual. How would the great figures of the various particular traditions have expressed *their* insights, had they been informed in a similarly plural religious way? Would we have seen a mutual cross-fertilization and enrichment of the vocabularies of different faiths, or a resolute rejection of such a blending, or would the ineffability of the various starting points automatically bankrupt any apparent enrichment which might have taken place?

The question of similarity and difference is insistently posed here, for, depending on the similarity or difference perceived between the various points of beginning — God, Brahman, Nirvana, Tao etc., so the use of a strict mono-faith vocabulary or a more polyglot linguistic resource must be judged appropriate. Some seem to be in little doubt that a similar experience is *interpreted* differently, and that once the underlying similarity is recognized the subsequent interpretation may be more wide-ranging. As Ninian Smart put it:

If religious experience is our ground of faith, then let us not be so narrow as to consider only the experiences of *our* tradition. . . . We *interpret* our experience. We clothe our intuitions in the vestments of one tradition, sometimes quite unconsciously. Who has seen the Virgin in Banares? What Sicilian saint or Scotch divine has seen the celestial Buddha?[26]

Others seem to move towards an opposite conclusion. Thus Karl Barth remarks:

It is . . . unthinking to set Islam and Christianity side by side. . . . In reality nothing separates them so radically as the different ways in which they appear to say the same thing – that there is only one God.[27]

Certainly, if ineffability is a key characteristic of religious beginnings, a state of inter-religious similarity might be given some credence simply from the fact that it is not immediately obvious how, logically speaking, two or three ineffable experiences *could*, in fact, be considered different. For, to allow any differentiation would surely be to demand some specifiable qualities on which it might be based – but this would negate the original claim to ineffability. Whatever conclusions are reached about inter-religious similarity and difference, the serious consideration of the varieties of human religiousness by a religiously multilingual individual is a phenomenon whose outcome seems likely to be of immense theological interest.

However, fascinating though it is to speculate about how an individual such as Cipher might see and describe the transcendent differently from someone located within a context of mono-faith informedness, a more pressing concern is to consider how the apprehension of religious beginnings, supposing that it did indeed come about, could help in solving his dilemma and bring him closer to a decision about commitment. For, once such points of beginning were reached, it is not easy to see how we could ascend the interpretative stream again – even allowing that we knew *which* interpretative stream was appropriate. If they are ineffable, how can these beginnings bear such wordy structures as are presented in the hall of mirrors? Can these ineffable points of origin really be thought to validate anything so concrete as the Buddhist or Hindu or Christian way of life? Or can they offer peace of mind themselves? How is the gulf to be bridged between what is said about religion and what remains unsayable, yet apparently fundamentally originative? How, for example, could Cipher move from the starting point and destination of Hindu religiousness, Brahman, the one before whom words recoil, to an extensively conceptualized Hindu view of life – even supposing he was returned to or towards Brahman by a process of passing over, focused on Hindu belief and practice? Or can we assume that by reaching such an originative locus the rest will somehow follow automatically?

Secondly: We might, perhaps, consider whether the beginnings towards which Cipher envisages a return might not be taken as possible means of accounting for continuity and diversity at least in an intra-religious if not in an inter-religious sense, thus going some way towards explaining why there is such a plurality of outlooks in the first place. If we compare any of the key originative terms of religion at the dawn of a particular tradition's history and at the present moment, it appears that most ancient and most recent notions of 'God', for example, seem to differ in many respects. Yet, by and large, theologians firmly maintain that, in some way, it is a single and unchanging entity with which we are dealing throughout the history of a particular tradition. Unless we can point to some common element which is both specific enough to create some binding *sense* of tradition, of particular religious identity, yet never completely expressed by any specific attempt at expression, thus continually demanding new attempts to apprehend it, then, given the widely differing views of, for example, 'God' within the Christian tradition, it is difficult to see how we could be sure that in fact they all did stem from the same source and *were* talking about the same thing. The radical unlikeness at the beginning, the non-comparability of the religious starting point could provide a common element with just the required characteristics: it could be what all the accounts attempt to net within the offered interpretations/descriptions. It could be what remains constant – constantly elusive, yet constantly generative of attempts to apprehend it throughout a history of consequent diversity. On this view 'ineffable' acts precisely as what I. T. Ramsey termed a 'qualifier',[28] whose presence in religious language serves to 'multiply models without end'.[29] If we want to see the different models as belonging to a *single* interpretative stream, we must surely posit some such feature as the radical unlikeness of the religious beginning, if any sort of continuity is to be maintained. Whether this can be of use in explaining only intra-religious diversity, or if it could, perhaps, be extended to the inter-religious realm as well, is uncertain – though in some ways it is tempting to think of Hinduism, Buddhism, Judaism, Christianity, Islam and so on, as all being several attempted models of a persistently elusive master-image.

Thirdly: If the points of beginning are as radically unlike other experience as the quotations we considered earlier would seem to suggest, and if he succeeds in reaching them, then Cipher will be left with an interesting logical problem which will, at some stage, require attention. As J. L. Austin once pointed out, 'like' is 'the main flexibility device by whose aid, in spite of our limited vocabulary, we can always avoid being left completely speechless.'[30] According to Austin, 'like' provides the linguistic equivalent of being able to shoot round corners.[31] In other words, we can always say what something is like, even if it seems to be quite inexpressible in a more direct sense. But God, Brahman, Tao etc. seem to deny all application of likeness and leave us speechless. The problem then becomes how we can actually be *aware of* anything so entirely beyond the reach of all comparison. Whereas we can easily make sense of something which is unseeable – clearly we cannot see a child's cry or the scent of a rose – we cannot do likewise with the unsayable. Something which is not visible may be felt or smelled or touched or heard, but something which is not sayable, which is not like anything, by what means could we ever come to be aware of such a thing? As W. T. Stace put it:

If the mystical consciousness were absolutely ineffable, then we could not say so because we should be unconscious of such an experience.[32]

If Cipher did manage to experience the ineffable he would, one would hope, be in a better position to explain the apparent logical impossibility of having done so than is the anticipating onlooker. Indeed he would be well placed, from both a religious and logical point of view, to provide some sort of clarifying account of the varieties of religious ineffability, if we can allow that variety can exist here in the first place.

Finally, lest we think, in light of these problems, that Cipher's intended return to beginnings might be better characterized as heading nowhere, as being rather like Svetaketu's splitting of the seed from the banyan tree in terms of being left with nothing tangible, we ought, perhaps, to stress the apparent religious fecundity of *silence*, that attitude of mind which is appropriate in face of the ineffable. Thus in *The Religious Imagination and the Sense of God*, John Bowker looks at key points in four major religious traditions – Judaism, Christianity, Islam and Buddhism – in which the operative sense of God comes into crisis, but leads on from there to new ways of thinking about the transcendent. In each case, central figures are reduced to silence in some 'crisis of plausibility'[33] out of which is born a new way of looking at things. The four key points are:

Job, accepting silence before the apparent majesty of God, Jesus, choosing silence before his accusers, Muhammad in silence on Mount Hira (a silence later recapitulated by al-Ghazali when he stood in front of his university class and found himself unable to speak) and Gautama, the Buddha, electing silence after his enlightenment. ... Four quadrant points of silence, in each of which a transaction occurred in the prevailing characterization of God.[34]

If silence and the ineffable seem at times to be dead ends from where we cannot progress beyond logical conundrums and practical paralysis, at other times precisely such starting points seem to have acted as new beginnings of an intensely creative kind, in terms of evolving concepts of peace of mind. Whatever outcome lies in wait for Cipher, he might, perhaps, take to heart some advice given in the *Bhagavad Gita*. It seems strangely appropriate to his circumstances:

With reason armed with resolution, let the seeker quietly lead the mind into the Spirit, and let all his thoughts be silence.[35]

6

The Skull on the Mantel and the Burden of Goodness

The image of the skull on the mantel, which forms the first part of the title of this chapter, is taken from Thornton Wilder's description of a philosophers' club in Edinburgh. Whether Wilder's account, given in his novel *The Eighth Day*, is purely fictional or not, I simply do not know. But the historicity of the image does not much matter in terms of the way in which it can be applied to investigating a situation of religious plurality. According to Wilder, the club's members met for the purpose of discussing beliefs both past and present. Such discussions were, however, carried out in a strictly objective tone, enforced by a total prohibition on talking in the first or second person of the present tense. As a reminder of the rule and as a punishment for those who infringed it, a skull stood grimly on the mantel and into it all offenders who inadvertently spoke of what I or you believe, were required to place a fine.[1]

The image of the burden of goodness, which completes my title, is taken from a book by Huston Smith on, and entitled, *The Purposes of Higher Education*. According to Smith:

If there are things that ought to be believed, this being the whole meaning of truth, there are also sides that *ought* to be espoused: this is the burden of goodness. To remain neutral in the face of these, or to be over-hesitant in deciding where they lie, is not wisdom but its opposite.[2]

I will use these two powerful images, *the skull on the mantel* and *the burden of goodness*, to identify the two magnetic poles of opposite attraction between which Cipher's experience of the hall of mirrors seems to hover uneasily. On the one hand, Cipher must find out what others believe and why they do so, he must explore the various worlds of religious meaning which make up the hall of mirrors – and to do so effectively he must not allow his own premature evaluations to cloud the issue. Yet, on the other hand, he must try to come to some decision of his own about how *he* ought to view the world and, in consequence, how he ought to live his life. Given the extent of his awareness of religious outlooks and his craving for peace of mind, for some sense-giving account of the world, there is clearly a risk that he may either forget about uplifting the burden of goodness in the effort to survey the different varieties of possible load, or that he might be panicked into picking up a burden somewhat haphazardly, without giving due attention to its credentials. How can Cipher resolve the apparent tension between neutrality and commitment, between the need for someone in his situation to *explore* the hall of mirrors and his desire to reach a conclusion about what he sees there? How can he keep a proper balance between the skull on the mantel, with its insistence on maintaining an uninvolved investigative stance in which subjective feelings do not intrude, and the burden of goodness, with its insistence on personal involvement? Given the extent of possible alternatives, making any *particular* commitment seems threatened with indefinite postponement as each possibility is subjected to a process of investigation; given the strength of his need for some sense-giving outlook on the world, the extended investigation of possibilities which seems to be required *may* be threatened with curtailment in favour of some decisive acceptance. How, in the context of the hall of mirrors, is Cipher to ensure that whatever position of commitment he may arrive at, it is not premature, yet that the investigative process undertaken in search of a decision is not endlessly prolonged? The aim of this chapter is to explore this tension between neutrality and commitment and to see if, from Cipher's point of view, it may be resolved constructively.

To begin with, it is important to clarify what is meant by 'neutrality' in each of the two senses in which it is being used – for it is a word which without some elaboration is, perhaps, rather prone to encouraging unhelpful interpretations of what it means.

First, it has been stressed from the outset that Cipher is 'neutral' as regards the various religious outlooks on the world which he perceives in the hall of mirrors. Indeed, his situation has, on occasions, been referred to simply as that of 'neutral informedness' or 'informed neutrality'. In *this* sense 'neutrality' refers to Cipher's formally uncommitted stance as regards any religious position. He does not consider himself to be Hindu, Buddhist, Muslim, Christian or Jew. At the same time, though, he has not rejected Hinduism, Buddhism, Islam and so on as possible sources of the peace of mind he seeks. He simply has not yet made up his mind about them. Cipher is well-informed about the teachings of the various religions, but has not yet reached any conclusions about where he stands in relation to them. He is, for example *au fait* with Hindu ideas on rebirth, with the notion of no-self in Buddhism and with the Christian concept of a loving creator deity, to name but a few fragments from some of the images he sees in the hall of mirrors; but he has reached no decision about how accurately these – and a host of other pictures – address and reflect the nature of his existence and provide blueprints for the way he ought to live. He does not know whether or not to believe in the existence of God, or if he ought to think of himself as a reincarnating entity, or if, in some sense, he has no self. He does not know if any of the elements of his religious informedness, whether singly or in combination, accurately reflect his situation so that he should live his life according to the outlook they suggest. That is, he is unsure whether or not to commit himself to accepting any religious view of things.

In his interesting study of the logic of dialogue among religions, William A. Christian has remarked that, 'as a generalization, it seems fair to say that the major religions all present and teach patterns of life'.[3] The trouble is, the patterns which are suggested seem – at least at first sight – to be very different. Cipher, a child of the modern age in religious studies, and heir to a massive accumulation of information about the world's religions, can, as he looks around the hall of mirrors, see many different life-patterns suggested. His neutrality with regard to them means that he does not act as if any of them were true, but nor does he dismiss them as being false.

He is religiously neutral in the sense of being *undecided* or *non-aligned*. Neutrality in this first sense *must not be seen as some form of covert commitment*. Cipher is not a neutralist, someone who actively favours a neutral position. On the contrary, he actively seeks an abandonment of a neutrality which is unwanted. Given his feelings of insignificance, mystery and meaninglessness – his sense of lostness in the world – he wants to arrive at a position at which he may say with confidence of any offered antidote: 'Yes, it's effective, I will accept it, it's true,' or, 'No, this particular form of religiousness is of no relevance to me.' Nor must Cipher's unwanted neutrality be seen as constituting any absence of information about, or interest in, religion. The context in which Cipher's neutrality is set, and within which he will try to end it, is one of extensive information about and interest in religion.

Moreover, being neutral in this first sense does not mean that Cipher will have no likes or dislikes, or that he will not have been brought up in a particular social setting and be influenced by certain assumptions embedded in his culture and expressed by his peer-group. Indeed, in the loose sense of social milieu, he may even belong to some 'religious' grouping – though such a 'belonging' is not in any sense a genuine commitment. It could not, by any stretch of the imagination, qualify as the decision towards which his energies are directed. In short, 'neutrality' in this first sense is not intended to suggest that Cipher is some sort of ill-informed, opionless zombie confronting the world with an open-mouthed and empty-minded blankness which is content to remain blank. Cipher's zero, one resonance of meaning in his name which should be stressed, refers simply to his present position vis-a-vis *commitment* to religion, it is not meant to suggest that he is some sort of hollow man.

In his Wilde Lectures of 1972, published as *The Sense of God*, John Bowker has, I think correctly, spoken of the exploration of human behaviour in ways which appear to be open to a novelist alone.[4] That Cipher may be in danger of appearing as a 'hollow man', that he has not been developed into a full-bodied fictional character, but rather has been left as a shell of ideas, has to do with his emergence on the stage of a brief academic book, *not* with how his character ought actually to be envisaged. There is a definite argument to be made for suggesting that an exploration of his situation might have been better conducted via a quite different medium – as indeed there is a case for suggesting that religious studies might utilize much more the general form of the novel in the course of its investigations. However, this is simply not a medium I feel competent to employ.

Secondly, quite a different sense of 'neutrality' comes into play once a method such as passing over is brought into operation – and, unless we suppose Cipher to be possessed of a full personality and an ordinary biography, it may be difficult to see some of the things to which such neutrality refers. 'Neutrality' in this second sense is concerned with keeping in check and under firm control those various likes and dislikes which might prompt Cipher to an instant warming to, or cold-shouldering of, some religious outlook before he has had a chance to investigate it properly, so that he can come to see it as it is seen by those who live their lives according to its vision (and whose lives are thus contributory to, or constitutive of, the reflection which Cipher perceives). Neutrality in this sense, far from being something unwanted, is a deliberately cultivated state of mind which Cipher will adopt in the process of that investigation which he will embark on so that his neutrality in the first sense, that is, his indecision about commitment, may be ended. This second form of neutrality is an attempt to ensure that Cipher does not arrive at *premature* judgements, which are based on his failing to see, with sufficient depth and accuracy, the nature of those various worlds of religious meaning about which he wishes to reach an evaluative decision.

In attempting to be neutral in this second sense, two main sets of potentially obscuring factors will need to be set to one side, or bracketed out, or be in some way acknowledged as exerting an unwanted influence, thus requiring appropriate counter-measures to be taken.

First, various social and personal value judgements which are not *specifically* related to religion but which might, nonetheless, cloud Cipher's attempted perception of other worlds of religious meaning, will need to be acknowledged and 'neutralized'. For example, being a twentieth century Westerner, he will doubtless be accustomed to wearing shoes, shirt, collar and tie and to eating with cutlery. Such customs may, however, extend their significance to viewing those who dress in robes, or go barefoot, or eat with their fingers, as in some way being inferior. Clearly if such an assumption was allowed free rein it would not help Cipher to come to a close sharing of, say, the Buddhist monk's outlook on the world, dressed as he would be in saffron robes, walking in all probability barefoot and eating rice with his fingers from a wooden bowl. Similarly, Cipher may have some such personal idiosyncracy as, say, mistrusting people whose rate of blinking is faster than his own, or finding chanting – of whatever sort – ridiculous. Again, such assumptions will have to be set to one side if his passing over is not to be brought up sharp by obstacles of his own making.

Secondly, those social or personal judgements which relate directly to religion and which may act to cloud any view of this area of human experience beyond that which they already look out on, must, similarly, be acknowledged and steps taken towards their neutralization during the course of passing over. In Cipher's case the methodological neutrality demanded by this sort of approach will call for the bracketing out of, the attempt to lay to one side or to see through, his neutrality as regards religious commitment, neutrality in the *first* sense described. For if Cipher is to share, say, a Buddhist vision of the world, it is unlikely that his efforts to do so would come to much if all along he was thinking to himself: 'This is all very interesting, but I just don't know whether to believe it or not'. It is worth stressing again that 'passing over' is similar in many ways to acting. In just the same way as the actor who could not overcome an aversion to Scottish accents, or the feeling that anyone who believed in witches was feeble minded, or whose contempt for that bloody nobleman's code of conduct did not allow him to imagine just how vaulting ambition can be, might not get very far in a portrayal of Macbeth, so Cipher's ability to stand shoulder to shoulder with Hindu, Buddhist, Christian, Jew and Muslim and look out on the world as they perceive it, may likewise be frustrated if he cannot control the intrusion of premature evaluations. To go back to that old Red Indian saying mentioned in Chapter 4 as summing up the ethos of passing over, namely: 'do not judge a man until you have walked a mile in his mocassins', 'neutrality' in the second sense in which I am using the word simply has to do with the effort to take off our own shoes before embarking on such an exercise.

In his interesting – and indeed pioneering – work on methodology in the study of religion (for it was published as early as 1901) Morris Jastrow identified what he termed 'the personal equation'. 'So strong is this factor,' he wrote, 'that it is perhaps impossible to eliminate it altogether, but it is possible, and indeed essential, to keep it in check and under safe control.'[5] That much the same point was emphasized by many participants at the International Association for the History of Religion's conference on methodology held in Finland in 1973,[6] confirms both Jastrow's status as a pioneer and the importance of this element, in particular the need to control it, in religious studies. The attempt to impose neutrality in this second sense is simply an attempt to harness the personal equation, so that the investigator may approach outlooks different from that which he already holds, with empathy rather than antipathy. Obviously it is not possible, nor indeed desirable, to neutralize the personal equation in the sense of removing it permanently – to attempt to do so would bring a new meaning to the term 'character assassination'. What we are referring to here is simply an attempt to hold as much of it as possible in suspense for the duration of the inquiry. In a sense, referring back to the central metaphor of chapter 4, this sort of neutrality stresses the fact of our being in the same house in order that we have a common basis from which to explore each other's different outlooks, it brackets out temporarily our different worlds.

The problem is that passing over, in making sure that the personal equation is not *prematurely* aligned, will stress the common denominator of the human situation, rather than any particular reading of it – in order to investigate and evaluate those particular readings. Such neutrality, whilst necessary if we are to prevent unthinking acceptance of the status quo or a general leaping to conclusions, would also seem to have the potential of acting against *ever* uplifting a burden of goodness. Commitment seems, paradoxically, to be postponed, seemingly indefinitely, by a neutrality which has been adopted in order to reach it.

'Neutrality' is, perhaps, an unfortunate choice of word for both the senses in which I am using it. Indeed, that I use it at all has more to do with a tradition of such usage than with any personal endorsement of its suitability. In the first sense of neutrality, 'pre-commitment' might have been a less misleading label for Cipher's state of mind; whilst in the second sense, 'non-biased' rather than 'neutral' might well be preferred. 'Neutral' suggests in one context something clinical, inhuman and machine-like, in another something not in gear, and in a third sense presupposes a situation of conflict from which we have decided to remain aloof. None of these connotations is particularly helpful and we would, perhaps, do better to follow Basil Mitchell's advice and instead of talking about neutrality at all, simply 'register our *commitment* to conventions of free, fair and disciplined debate'[7] (for this is precisely what Cipher's situation seems to require). However, since I am not going to swim against the tide of linguistic convention by adopting a new vocabulary, I have simply qualified and explained my use of 'neutrality'.

It is also as well to be clear on some of the senses 'neutrality' is *not* being taken to have. In particular, there are two possible misunderstandings of what the neutrality required in passing over involves which it is especially important to avoid.

First, the neutrality required in order to effect the return to beginnings which Cipher seeks does not constitute an attempt to reach some sort of presuppositionless starting point. Cipher's deliberate efforts to be neutral do not mean that he is attempting to achieve some kind of *tabula rasa* upon which may then be written the results of his explorations, uninfluenced by any extraneous factors. Anders Nygren has strongly condemned the confusion between prejudice and presupposition which lies at the heart of supposing that neutrality involves the annihilation of everything the investigator thought or believed beforehand, in the interests of a supposedly uncontaminated methodology. The desire for such antiseptic conditions of investigation overlooks the rather basic fact that the process of sterilization involved, even if it were possible to achieve, would kill off any intelligible process of inquiry as well as those germs of prejudice which might indeed threaten to influence its results. Nygren points out that, whilst 'prejudice' conveniently means exactly what its etymology suggests, namely, that an opinion has been formed before (*prae*) the case has been brought to trial (*judicium*), that judgement has been reached without looking at the evidence, the common usage of 'presupposition' tends to lose sight of the fact that presuppositions refer to those funda-mental and unquestionable assumptions on which the ability to make judgements in the first place depends. To use the instances Nygren cites: we presuppose that there is a distinc-tion between true and false and between good and evil. In *Meaning and Method*, Nygren goes so far as to suggest that the confusion between prejudice and presupposition has reached such proportions that it must be regarded as 'a cultural menace'.[8] He argues that:

When the presuppositions on which all thought and cultural life rest come to be described as 'prejudices' which we could well do without, this is no longer merely a harmless linguistic confusion but some-thing with far-reaching consequences in every direction.[9]

One of those consequences would be to render quite absurd the methodological pre-requisites of passing over – for whilst it is one thing to seek to control potentially prejudicial aspects of one's outlook, it is quite something else to attempt to obliter-ate one's presuppositions in an indiscriminate jettisoning which lumps them together with prejudice. In a fascinating essay on anamnesis and belief, J. J. Kim endorses Nygren's warnings. Making a presuppositionless starting point the prerequisite of an inquiry is, he says, an 'inhuman obsession', a 'Cartesian aberration' which has 'infected Western thought for centuries'.[10]

It is, I think, this sort of misunderstanding of what neutral-ity involves which can lead very easily to an interpretation of the skull on the mantel as something representing a bleak indictment of attempts to examine religion from a neutral standpoint, rather than simply as constituting a reminder or recommendation of a neutral element in methodology. As the mood in religious studies has changed from primitivism to modernism, from a dismissive judgemental approach which operated an *a priori* negative evaluation on 'other' outlooks, to a non-judgemental investigative approach, the critic of such a process might point to the skull on the mantel as the *death's head* of neutrality, a death's head whose baleful medusa gaze, shorn of all expression of personal commitment, turns to stone each living faith it touches on and sums up graphically the lifelessness which exaggerated impartiality can lead to. Any attempt to study religion from a neutral position, so this interpretation would argue, does fatal violence to the subject matter. In such an approach, the gruesomely appropriate symbol of its own mistaken methodology simply stands for the fate which awaits the subject matter approached according to its deadening mores. If neutrality is allowed to extend into an 'inhuman obsession' where so much of the investigator's personality is bracketed out that, in the unlikely event of such a radical neutralization being possible, he would become a veritable zombie, then there seems to be no good reason to suppose that he would be equipped for anything except a massive *misapprehension* of religion – or of anything else. Perhaps it is fear of such a perversion of neutrality which fuels the idea that observer and believer stand on opposite sides of some great divide which all but the most minimal understanding is quite unable to cross. Although elsewhere in the same volume he has suggested that the roles of observer and believer may be starting to coalesce,[11] in a passage in *The Meaning and End of Religion*, Wilfred Cantwell Smith writes:

Heaven and hell, to a believer, are stupendous places into one or other of which he is about to step. To an observer they are items in the believer's mind. To the believer they are parts of the universe; to the observer they are parts of religion.[12]

The neutrality which Cipher 'naturally' possesses – neutrality in the first sense which I described, the fact of his indecision concerning commitment, means that heaven, hell, sunyata, nirvana, the tao, and other such sacred states or loci, across the vast reaches of a religious topography mapped out for him by religious studies, are *possibilities*, possibly stupendous places his relationship to which he has not yet decided. The neutrality which he will *deliberately* employ in passing over, in order to try to find out, neutrality in the second sense which I have described, does *not* mean that Cipher will suddenly become rather unconcerned, distanced and detached, in such a way that he will thereafter view such things as rather peculiar phenomena, of no particular interest to himself. All that the adoption of this sort of neutrality means is that he will attempt to see them clearly, so that he may reach a decision about them.

As Bernard E. Meland has shown, in his study of the relationship between theology and the history of religions, there is no such thing as a completely neutral inquiry, that is, an inquiry in which 'the interested, centred existence of the inquirer plays no part'.[13] Rather than aiming for something unreachable – and, indeed, undesirable – such as total neutrality, Cipher will aim for something very like the position which Meland goes on to characterize as possible and useful, where 'the biases of interest and conditioning are brought *reasonably* under control'.[14] Self-awareness and self-understanding, according to Meland's analysis, are importantly contributory towards making such a disciplined effort effective.

Cipher, like the historian, must learn to curb a self-centredness that is, as Arnold Toynbee put it, 'one of the intrinsic limitations and imperfections of all life',[15] he must 'consciously and deliberately (shift) his angle of vision away from the initial self-centred standpoint natural to him as a living creature'[16] if, that is, he is to see how others have seen the world. Unless he does this, he will simply remain incapable of responding to other points of view and, as such, will see only a single reflection in the hall of mirrors. In so doing, he might, incidentally, as Toynbee has observed, be making a *moral* as well as an intellectual mistake.[17] But such a shift in viewpoint does not involve some sort of erasure of personality so that an impersonal, camera-eye's outlook may be adopted, it simply attempts to neutralize those aspects of his existing vision which may distort what he wants to see beyond it.

Stanley A. Cook, who, along with Morris Jastrow, is one of the pioneers in the methodology of the study of religion, noted how the 'ultra-impartial mind that drifts away from its values, that has not firm elementary principles',[18] is, in fact, wholly unsuited for conducting an inquiry into religion. Just as acting requires the imaginative flexibility of a *full* human personality in which *prejudices* are carefully laid aside, so passing over requires the presence of the complete person, with certain aspects of the personality deliberately controlled, not some sort of methodological ghost.

The second possible misunderstanding of 'neutrality' which it is important to correct, imagines that by adopting a methodological neutrality to render passing over effective, Cipher will lose the ability to judge and discriminate between those areas on which he will base his passing over. 'Neutrality' is taken to mean that he must accept on equal terms everyone who calls themself Christian or Hindu or Buddhist, because to do otherwise would allow in an element of obscuring judgement and evaluation. Far from involving any lack of *discernment*, as this misunderstanding of neutrality seems to think an attempt to control the personal equation will entail, those expressions of individual religiousness whose outlook on the world he will attempt to share will be drawn from a *selected* group. Just as it would be easy enough to dismiss music as something trite and silly if one only listened to its trivial manifestations, so too, it would be easy for Cipher to dismiss religion out of hand as irrelevant to his quest for peace of mind, if he focused only on its ever-abundant mediocre representatives. And just as to limit the area of music which is to be given serious consideration is not to presume that Mahler or Wagner, Beethoven or Vivaldi is best, so one can likewise limit the area of interest in an inquiry into religion, without presuming that some single particular outlook is thereby to be favoured.

For example, Cipher would not be likely to get very far with his inquiries into the Christian outlook on the world, if he attempted to pass over to the perspective of the sort of Catholic described by Miguel de Unamuno. 'Strictly speaking in Spain today', wrote Unamuno in 1906,

to be a Catholic in the vast majority of cases, scarcely means more than not to be anything else. A Catholic is a man who, having been baptized, does not publicly abjure what is assumed, by a social fiction, to be his faith; he does not think about it one way or the other, either to profess it or reject it, either to take up another faith, or even to seek one.[19]

Unamuno's comment identifies a common category of nominal believer which extends religiously far beyond Catholicism and, geographically and historically, far beyond Spain in the early 1900s. Such nominal believers, unlike Cipher, are indeed neutral about religion in a somewhat zombie-like manner. Saying that Cipher would not get very far in his inquiries into the Christian outlook on the world if his passing over were to be focused on such believers, is not, of course, to infer from their somewhat uninspiring attitude that the God of their nominal belief does not exist, or that Christianity is to be rejected lock, stock and barrel because of the unconvincing way in which they present it as being a legitimate source of peace of mind. Taking an example rather closer to home, John Bowker has shown that although the behaviour of Catholics and Protestants in Northern Ireland may suggest that 'the claimed object of their belief has no specifiable reality *in effect*',[20] i.e. that their inter-action often seems to be particularly godless, this 'does not in itself provide a comment on the reality of the objects of their belief'.[21] Doubtless, even from the most peripheral expressions of Christian religiousness, Cipher could eventually penetrate to the heart of the matter, unless the connections with it were so tenuous as to be indistinguishable from actual severment. It would, however, seem perverse to start off at the furthest remove from the goal which is being sought. Cipher's dilemma might be more adequately served, if his passing over was directed to those examples of religiousness which seem to let on directly into the arterial system of a particular faith. Neutrality does not preclude the selecting for study of those cases which seem closest to the heart.

Given the importance of choosing the area to which his passing over will be directed – or, if you like, of choosing those points of entry into a religious structure which will allow him quick access to its arterial system, Cipher might well spend some time considering what criteria to use in assessing who counts as a good Christian, a good Buddhist, a good Hindu and so on – i.e. who constitute good examples of these sorts of religiousness at the peak of their credibility. Some guidelines will, obviously, be afforded by the religions themselves. But it is interesting to consider whether any inter-religious criteria of value might be available here. I suppose that in a sense what Cipher is looking for is religious *maturity*, he is looking for the image of Jewish or Islamic religiousness at the peak of its development, he is interested in finding out – as James Fowler puts it in his seminal work *Stages of Faith* – 'what developmental trajectory into mature faith is envisioned and called for by a particular faith tradition at its best.'[22] If he can plot out such trajectories accurately, then clearly he will be able to direct his passing over towards those examples of religiousness where the heart of the matter beats most strongly and visibly. Interestingly, in Fowler's analysis of faith development, the final and most mature of the six stages of faith which he identifies – what he calls 'universalizing faith', which may occur within any particular religious context – is 'often experienced as subversive of the structures (including religious structures) by which we sustain our individual and corporate survival, security and significance'.[23] In consequence, 'many persons at this stage die at the hands of those whom they hope to change', (Gandhi and Martin Luther King being two of the modern examples which he cites).[24] The *subversiveness* which fully mature faith may display towards accepted norms of behaviour is a timely reminder that the peace of mind apparently offered by religion is something of a misnomer. As Harvey Cox rather neatly put it with regard to one particular formula for peace of mind, 'seriously following the God of Israel', (and of course that 'seriously' needs to be emphasized in order to separate it from the tagging along of nominal allegiance), 'can play havoc with one's social roles'.[25]

If passing over is an attempt to return to religious beginnings, and if it was successful in returning Cipher to a point of close proximity to whatever originative locus of transcendence lies at the source of the particular image he is investigating, then surely there is little need to worry about resolving any tension which might occur between neutrality and commitment. Will the problem not be solved automatically if his investigations take him to, or even sufficiently *towards*, the heart of the matter? Will he not, so to speak, be pulled into its magnetic field, and his commitment follow as a matter of course? Going back to Kristensen's comments on the investigation of Islam, which were mentioned in Chapter 5, if Cipher came to perceive the reality in question, namely Allah, would he not then uplift the Islamic 'burden of goodness' and be or become a Muslim? And would this not constitute a natural conclusion to his quest, such that the unwanted neutrality of his indecision about the different worlds of religious meaning would be replaced by a commitment to one particular outlook, and the neutrality required by passing over could, like the process itself, be considered redundant, having served its purpose?

This takes us back into an area of uncertainty regarding the *outcome* of a process of passing over, and that uncertainty is, as I have suggested, best discussed after a serious attempt has been made actually to follow its methodological guide-lines. However, if Cipher did find himself drawn sufficiently close to the heart of Islam or Christianity or Hinduism to become a committed Muslim, Christian or Hindu, it is important to point out that although the tensions between neutrality and commitment, between the apparently conflicting imperatives issued by the skull on the mantel and the burden of goodness, might then *seem* to be resolved, they would, in a sense, just have been transferred to a different area. Instead of being a problem for the uncommitted Cipher, it would become a matter of *theological* concern addressed to his new religiously committed role. For could a standpoint from within any of the particular faith-territories simply close its eyes to the existence of the adjoining religious terrain? Surely as religious information intrudes into the purview of a particular faith-stance it must investigate it – if only to establish if there is any common ground between them, to find out if the religious terrain is co-terminous across areas of different spiritual habitat, or if such habitats are, in fact, islands with no underlying connections. But, if such investigation is required, then presumably neutrality will still be needed in the subsequent exploration – otherwise the whole thing could be solved in advance by juggling with a series of theological *a prioris*. Thus, even within a particular stance of commitment, the tension between neutrality and commitment seems to remain.

The opposing influences of the skull on the mantel and the burden of goodness seem likely thus to extend even into any position of commitment which Cipher's quest might reach. Does this mean that there can be no constructive resolution of the tension between them, that such a tension is simply a permanent feature of a world which is perceived to be religiously plural, so that no resting place of finally satisfactory commitment can ever be reached?

The tension will, in fact, only cause a sense of strain if neutrality and commitment are understood in what I would argue are very questionable ways. If neutrality is taken as a virtual erasure of personality such that, by adopting it, one would approach religion with indifference rather than impartiality, and if commitment is taken as a single decisive act of acceptance and allegiance which would brook no subsequent process of reflection, then, obviously, there would be considerable tension felt when any effort was made to think about religion.

But, if neutrality is seen as a device for trying to ensure that we arrive at the truth, and commitment is seen as an attempt to live according to whatever truth is perceived, then there would seem to be no particular difficulty in allowing that the two attitudes of mind, far from occupying contradictory positions, are very much part of the same continuum of moral seriousness. Northrop Frye provides us with a useful reminder of the moral dimension to the sort of neutrality required by passing over.

The persistence in keeping the mind in a state of disciplined sanity, the courage in facing results that may deny or contradict everything that one had hoped to achieve – these are moral qualities if the phrase means anything at all.[26]

If we envisage commitment as being the adoption of a very narrow and clearly defined outlook, which acts to close the mind to any subsequent information or reflection which might amend or challenge it, then the demands of the skull on the mantel seem wholly incompatible with the rather uncomfortable burden of goodness thus uplifted. But, if commitment is envisaged as a rather more open state of mind, then it is surely more accurate to see the skull on the mantel as part of – and, indeed, an important and very weighty part of – whatever burden of goodness we decide to carry.

Joseph McClelland has suggested that this kind of open commitment involves

a critical attitude towards one's own commitment so that one moves between the poles of subjectivity and objectivity, or theology and religious studies, passion and apathy, or however we indicate the tension aroused by thinking about living.[27]

Whilst I am a little unsure of some of the implications of McClelland's list of contrasting but complementary pairs, I think his remark is quite accurate in identifying *thinking about living* as the cause of tension within any *particular* outlook on life. So long as the Hindu or the Christian or the Buddhist continues to think about life, it is hard to see how their religious commitment, if it were to deny the intellectual mobility which is facilitated by neutrality, could become anything but static, uncritical and uninvolved in such thought.

The idea of 'open' commitment raises all kinds of interesting questions about the finality or provisionality of any particular form of religiousness, and about in what ways becoming a Buddhist is significantly different from becoming a Christian or a Muslim and, moreover, what it means to 'become' religious in the first place. Such questions, like so many others I have side-stepped, will only be properly ans-

wered when the inter-relationship between the different religions is clearly mapped, and their similarities and differences
firmly established.

Although 'open' commitment may involve a loss of dogma-
tic certainty, as this can be expressed within the confines of a
single faith which never looks beyond its own boundaries, the
inter-religious exploration it will encourage can, in fact, be
seen as *strengthening* rather than weakening one's religious
position. As Robert McDermott has put it, adapting the
famous Socratic dictum:

once it is admitted that 'the unexamined religious position is not
worth living', then a critical reading of one's own religious faith and
tradition ... aided by the study of another position – must be
considered an ideal as well as a responsibility.[28]

It is, as McDermott acknowledges, impossible to predict just
what affect one's study of another religious position will have
on one's own, since unlike matching it against a critical
scientific or philosophical outlook which may question it at
specific points, the value and challenge of contrasting faith
with faith is that sympathetic understanding of another religious tradition 'reveals an alternative for every part of one's
religion'.[29] Although the outcome of such a process is, as
McDermott says, uncertain, it is interesting to note that, in
one passing over which must, presumably, be of considerable
interest to Christian and Buddhist theologian alike, Harvey
Cox has shown how it is not, apparently, impossible to
strengthen and deepen a Christian religiousness by learning
from, and even adopting, various Buddhist practices.[30]

James Fowler has drawn attention to the risk of precocious
identity formation if children are exposed at an early age to
insistent religious fundamentalism.[31] The premature voicing
of adult-endorsed opinion which results in such situations
is very much a case of words being parroted, without any
understanding of the concepts which they are meant to con-
vey. More generally, when young people, either through
choice or undue influence, take on the values and life-styles of
their parents without question, they enter an identity-status

which James Marcia has aptly termed 'foreclosure'.[32] In the context of the hall of mirrors there seems to be a risk of what we might call *religious foreclosure*, when a position of closed commitment is adopted and the role of neutrality in allowing extensive mental mobility is denied. Such a position of foreclosure, of premature commitment, might seem at first sight to solve Cipher's dilemma, but it would be a response to the many different religious lights which confuse him which had recourse to blinkering, rather than genuinely seeing a way through.

It is easy to run from the spectre of neutrality, conceived of as a deadening, destructive force, into the arms of a situation where closed commitment seems to offer the alternative of religious security. From Cipher's point of view, such a retreat would, however, involve no more than a changing of valueless money from a bankrupt methodology to a bankrupt position of commitment. Given his situation of multi-religious informedness, neither indifference nor dogmatism offers an acceptable way out. Perhaps, if my metaphorical camel will stand a few more interpretative straws, the image of the skull on the mantel, *understood as an intrinsic part of each burden of goodness which Cipher is faced with*, might be taken to stand for the demise of those varieties of narrowly particularized faiths whose secure singularity is afforded only by a refusal to look around them.

Finally, we might note that certain basic facts of anatomy redeem the skull from any purely funereal function which our first emotional reactions to it are likely to infer. For, quite apart from the more dramatic and imaginative aspects which have become associated with it, the skull is – quite simply – the necessary foundation for the face and the protection for the brain which gives sense to any expression which that face might make. Perhaps, in the end, any skull which Cipher places on his mantel should simply act as a reminder that, in order to arrive at a proper understanding of a religion, we must remember that there is more to it than meets the eye, more to it than the superficiality of surface smiles and scowls, but that, to get beyond the level of the obvious, we must pass through much that may be difficult to penetrate and indeed frightening to behold. Such a passage will not be possible if we are shackled immovably to a burden of unreflective dogmatism which we have mistaken for something more worthwhile, or if, through seeking some sort of *total* neutrality, we attempt to absent ourselves from the audience of humanity which all religions address.

7

Some Concluding Reflections

In *Ascent of the Mountain, Flight of the Dove*, a book which he sub-titles 'An Invitation to Religious Studies', Michael Novak writes:

Religion is a conversion from the ordinary, given, secure world into a world of nothingness, terror, risk – a world in which, nevertheless, there is a strange healing joy.[1]

It is into Cipher's ordinary, given, secure world of day to day experience that feelings of insignificance, mystery and meaninglessness intrude, so that it becomes *insecure* and he feels the need for some sort of curative peace of mind, or what Novak terms a 'strange healing joy'. We have been concerned with exploring how his quest for such a thing might best be conducted in the context of a religiously plural world where many *possible* senses of security are apparently available.

At the end of the last chapter it was suggested that one interpretation of the image of the 'skull on the mantel' was to see it as a reminder of the fact that, if we are to progress beyond a somewhat superficial view of religion, we must pass through much that may be difficult to understand and frightening to behold. Novak's remark serves as a useful reminder of this frightening aspect, of what we might term the dark side of religion, which is all too often glossed over or forgotten. It would, for example, be easy to see Cipher's intended quest in over-simplistic terms, as involving a motivating sense of insecurity or unease, which sends him scurrying towards the safe havens variously offered by religions.

But, although they do indeed offer such havens, religions also act to *accentuate* the sense of insecurity which desires them. The 'strange healing joy' of religion, the peace of mind which Cipher seeks – something which, as we have noted, seems to involve a purported relationship of closeness to ultimate reality – is offered in a perspective which also involves an increase in precisely those negative senses of insignificance, mystery and meaninglessness – Novak's nothingness, terror and risk – which will fuel and magnify Cipher's sense of lostness. Moreover, peace of mind may, from the point of view of everyday existence, seem to offer a calm which is unpleasantly turbulent.

To stress the way in which religious outlooks on the world seem with one hand to undermine any sense of everyday security, whilst with the other they offer a purportedly deeper sense of well-being, it is, perhaps, useful to draw a distinction between what we might term *mundane* and *world* aspects of certainty and uncertainty, remembering that the possibility of finding some form of *religious* world certainty, or peace of mind, or 'strange healing joy' – call it what you choose – is the whole focus of Cipher's interest in the hall of mirrors.

In stressing the double action of religion, fostering world *un*certainty and offering world certainty, we may gain further insight into what Cipher's environment is like and how it may, in fact, serve to give his quest an increasing sense of urgency. In particular, I want to develop the sense of world uncertainty given in Chapter 1, presenting it now as something intimately bound up with, if not identical to, a sense of lostness, rather than simply being a neutral position *vis-a-vis* commitment.

Mundane certainty is simply an acceptance of things as routine and everyday which does not probe beneath commonsense answers to questions of purpose, but sees them as sufficient in themselves. 'What is the purpose of your life?' 'What am I here for?' Mundane certainty will reply: 'to get a good job, to find somewhere pleasant to live and bring up a family, to become rich and famous, to travel round the world . . .', or in terms of whatever else may be considered to be a worthy goal.

World certainty, on the other hand, involves accepting an account of things which sees the commonplace against the backdrop of rather wider terms of reference. 'What is the purpose of your life?' 'What am I here for?' World certainty will reply: 'to escape from the eternal round of karma and rebirth, to follow the Eightfold Path and achieve Nirvana, to obey God's commandments, to follow the teachings of the Qur'an . . .', or in terms of whatever other world view is accepted. (I am, of course, confining myself to religious world certainties here, but we must remember that political or scientific terms of reference may also provide something similar.)

We might, perhaps, define a seriously committed religious life, as one in which day to day actions are performed in accordance with a view of ultimate meaning, which sees some significance in them over and above their immediately observable consequences; a non-religious life, as one in which day to day actions and ambitions are performed and followed without reference to any transcendent state or entity beyond themselves; and a nominal religious life, as one in which lip-service is paid to some point of transcendent reference which is then, to all intents and purposes, ignored.

Moving on to uncertainty: *Mundane uncertainty* is simply that doubt or indecision which questions specific elements in our experience: what career do we want to follow, how ought we to vote, where do we wish to live? . . . and so on.

World uncertainty, on the other hand, questions the sense of life itself and asks in a profound and basic way: what ought I to do? how ought I to lead my life? what should I believe about the world? and so on. *It is a state of mind where not only has no decision been reached about the overall meaning of things, but where the absence of such a decision is felt as a pressing deficiency which acts to undermine any sense of contentment.*

The desire for some form of world certainty occurs when we find our lives confronted by this disturbing feeling of undermining *un*certainty and indecision, which opens our eyes to how insignificant, mysterious and meaningless human life may at times appear to be, *unless* there are wider terms of reference to appeal to than those afforded by day to day existence. Cipher's sense of lostness is, precisely, a feeling of chronic world uncertainty.

Clearly for most of the time most of us *are* reasonably content to operate very much on the level of outlook offered by commonsense. We eat, sleep, read and write books and pursue whatever other business we are engaged in, without particularly worrying about issues of ultimate meaning and sense. But sometimes such a commonsense outlook simply does not seem sufficient. The mundane certainties and uncertainties which characterize much of our existence seem suddenly overtaken and transcended by issues of an altogether different scale.

The conditions under which world uncertainty assails us are many and varied. Although what Bourdillon and Fortes aptly term our 'threshold of vulnerability'[2] to the human situation has been raised enormously, so that we can now control and understand many of those phenomena which might otherwise have aroused a sense of world uncertainty much sooner, we are still sufficiently subject to the facts of birth, suffering and death, set in the context of an unpredictable future, an irretrievable past and an awing immensity of space, to wonder about the ultimate nature of our existence and the way in which it ought to be conducted.

Often, a sense of world uncertainty arises out of an encounter with suffering – some event which stresses our transient finitude, and seems to make a nonsense of any identity and rationale offered to us by considerations of occupation, intelligence, wealth, social standing and so on; or it may be triggered through encountering information about some variety of world *certainty*, which then calls into question the adequacy of any more mundane scheme of sense.

A great deal of literature is concerned with chronicling our attempts to cope in various ways with the impingement of world uncertainty upon our lives. In *Those Barren Leaves*, for example, a novel in which mundane certainty and world uncertainty are juxtaposed with great comic effect, Aldous Huxley has summed up well the relationship between these two sides of our humanity.

All one's daily life is a skating over thin ice, a scampering of water beetles across the invisible skin of depths. Stamp a little too hard, lean a shade too heavily and you are through, you are floundering in a dangerous and unfamiliar element.[3]

Mundane certainty and uncertainty form a thin skin over depths, and, fragile though the surface which they provide may seem to be, it bears the bulk of the weight of human movement. Cipher seems somehow to have stamped too hard or leant too heavily, so that he is less preoccupied with surface concerns than with plotting a course through the dangerous and unfamiliar element of *world* uncertainty which seems to him to underlie them. In looking at the different navigational possibilities, though, he is hardly likely to be reassured about the security of a mundane, surface existence.

Whether or not it is approached from the standpoint of an *existing* sense of world uncertainty such as Cipher possesses (to a deliberately exaggerated degree), the acquisition of information about the religions of the world is as likely to *increase* such a sense as it is to provide any antidote for it. It is one of the paradoxes of religion that it offers both fundamental certainty and uncertainty, a rich source of meaning and a formidable vision of what is meaningless. In order to set the stage upon which to present its sense-giving outlooks on the human condition, it must first stress the features of that condition which call out for its perspective in the first place. There would be no point in presenting a world certainty to an audience which was unshakeably satisfied with a mundane outlook on things. For religious perspectives rely on showing that meaninglessness, uncertainty and incompleteness characterize any life which is considered adequate without some sort of transcendent dimension.

A neutral informedness about religious teachings might thus be expected to *increase* that awareness of our existence which sees it as something dwarfed by the immensities of time and space and perpetually threatened with disruption by the prospect of seemingly random suffering and, eventually, by death. At the same time, such religious knowledge might be expected to offer details of various strategies of solace which might be adopted in the face of such a daunting outlook. Religion offers peace of mind to heal those wounds which consciousness may come to feel more keenly, precisely through an acquaintance with religious thinking. As Winston L. King put it:

One may generalize and say that religious traditions always go out of their way to paint life in its darkest colours and to stress the precariousness and evil condition of human existence. *Religion may be defined in this context as the awareness of a basic wrongness with the world and as the technique of dealing with that wrongness.*[4]

Or as Hocking put it rather more concisely, in *The Meaning of God in Human Experience*, religion may often be seen as 'the healing of a breach which religion itself has made'.[5]

Given his natural sense of world uncertainty, and the fact that this will, most probably, be strengthened and deepened by his experience of the religious outlooks found in the hall of mirrors, it is clear that Cipher's search for the possibility of peace of mind may be undertaken with an *increasing* sense of urgency. One of his key tasks must be to try to establish the extent to which the 'basic wrongness' perceived by the religious consciousness, as characterizing human existence, is, in fact, similarly diagnosed by Hinduism, Judaism, Buddhism, Christianity, Islam and so on, and if the techniques they offer for dealing with it may thus be seen as potential cures for the same ailment, or if different treatments are being offered for different aspects of the same disease or for different illnesses altogether. The completion of such a task will be one of the desired outcomes of the process of passing over.

Thus, there appears to be an almost certain *negative* outcome to Cipher's intended search for peace of mind, or world certainty, in the context of the hall of mirrors. Such an outcome is at direct variance with what he is seeking, for it entails an *increase* in precisely that which he wishes to minimize, indeed to lose altogether, namely, his sense of lostness. One conclusion it seems safe to draw is that, whatever the final outcome of his quest for peace of mind may be, his search for it in the religious hall of mirrors will involve, at least temporarily, a heightening of its exact opposite. For it is hard to see how, in such a context, he could avoid the 'massive religious sense of something wrong with the world'.[6] Can any similarly probable conclusions be drawn on a more *positive* note, concerning the likelihood of Cipher's actually finding some sort of curative peace of mind, which would act to silence the sense of lostness which his quest may otherwise simply exaggerate? Is it reasonable to suppose that Cipher will find the peace of mind he seeks, that he will find some envaluing religious integer behind which to place his zero of lostness? Or is it more likely that his search will be inconclusive, or that he will decide that no such thing as peace of mind exists?

The attempt to draw a firm conclusion after what has, we must remember, only been a preliminary discussion about methodology, would be quite misguided. At best, these seven chapters are the first part of a three-phase inquiry: the second phase would employ the technique of passing over on particular religious images, whilst the third would consider those critiques of religion which question its status as a locus of legitimate peace of mind, critiques which are voiced variously from psychological, philosophical and sociological perspectives. So, clearly it would be premature to end with a conclusion which should really only be made, and even then *tentatively*, at the end of some far-off, hypothetical twenty-first chapter. Rather than making any categorical conclusion of a definitive singular variety, I shall end our present shadowing of Cipher's footsteps with some anticipatory assessments which look forward to what seem from here to be *possible* outcomes of his quest in the hall of mirrors for what Novak calls religion's 'strange healing joy', or what I have termed 'peace of mind'. These assessments ought not to be allowed to obscure the fact that really the only appropriate conclusion which can be offered at this stage is, in a very real sense, '*Wait and see*'.

One assessment of the likely outcome of Cipher's intended quest for peace of mind in the religious hall of mirrors, sees it developing into an endless and increasingly laborious *going round in circles*, which takes him no nearer to any point of satisfactory conclusion than he was before he began. Indeed, if anything, he will be led progressively further and further away from reaching any conclusion with each additional orbit in which he turns. According to *this* anticipatory assessment, Cipher will set out from his situation of perplexed neutral informedness, on an investigative journey of the different images which he already has a surface awareness of, but his investigation, conducted via the process of passing over, will *not* take him any closer to some point of commitment. Rather, it will simply add to the perplexing information he already has, and so serve to deepen and perpetuate the problem until he can break the circle of information/ perplexity/ investigation : *increased* information/ *renewed* perplexity and so on. Moreover, not only will his intended quest increase his perplexity, in terms of expanding his awareness of the number of *possible* world certainties he might, in the end, adopt; such an awareness is, as we have seen, likely to have the effect of *increasing* his sense of lostness. Obviously, were this to be the outcome of his quest, Cipher would be likely to abandon the whole sphere of religion as being impenetrably problematic and unpleasantly disturbing. However, one slight note of encouragement might be sounded even if so apparently discouraging an outcome did, in fact, occur.

This note of encouragement simply takes the form of a reminder of the two senses in which 'hall' can be understood (something which was mentioned briefly in Chapter 1, in the details given there about the hall of mirrors). In one sense 'hall' is a place of transit, somewhere you pass through on route to where you wish to go, but definitely not somewhere to envisage spending any time. It has been this sense of 'hall' which has, very largely, been dominant in our considerations so far, so that *remaining* in the hall of mirrors would be seen as unsatisfactory. But a second sense of 'hall' understands it as referring to the main room in a great house, somewhere we might quite well consider to be a satisfactory destination. If this second sense is coupled to the idea of *open* commitment, suggested in Chapter 6, and if we allow that, increasingly, any particular expression of religiousness is likely to be set in the context of perceived plurality, then perhaps we ought not to view Cipher as being very much in transit, but, even if he does not feel he has reached his desired destination, more as at least occupying the proper milieu in which it will be set. Going round in circles may not be such a fruitless thing as it seems, if commitment itself is viewed in orbital rather than static terms. However, this is only a *slight* note of encouragement in what would still be an unsatisfactory situation. Whether it could be built up into something more substantially reassuring is uncertain.

A second assessment of the result of Cipher's intended quest sees its likely outcome as one of coming up against a brick wall, rather than going round in circles. In his thoughtful and stimulating essay on *The Purposes of Higher Education*, from which the notion of the burden of goodness was drawn, Huston Smith has argued that at the root of every subject area there are a few apparently simple questions, which regularly deflate its experts and threaten to bring their other inquiries to a halt, because such inquiries seem to be underlain, or rather *undermined*, by these simple questions, which, although they have logical priority over any subsequent inquiry, have remained substantially unanswered, and are, perhaps, unanswerable. For example, in education, according to Smith's analysis, each more specialized inquiry is underlain by the absolutely basic query which asks: 'What are we trying to do when we teach?'[7] or, put another way, 'What is education?'

So too for Cipher, there seems to be a sense in which any specific inquiry into Hindu, Buddhist, Jewish or Christian religiousness will be underlain by so many unanswered fundamental questions, that any conclusions he reaches must be viewed as significantly lacking in reliable foundations. To echo Smith's educational example: 'What are we trying to do when we become or are religious?' or, more simply, 'What is religiousness?' Add to this, questions which refer to the relationship between religions or to the criteria for judging religious outlooks as true or false, and all Cipher's small-scale endeavours seem quite overshadowed by a handful of massively simple, but difficult, questions. Whilst this kind of assessment is useful for reminding us of the importance of certain fundamental questions, it would, I think, be quite mistaken to assume that because they have been left unanswered, all subsequent inquiry is in some way devalued. Or, more specifically, that because Cipher has not answered them they will form an impenetrable wall, upon which all his other endeavours are fated to break. For it is surely misleading to think of such questions as being initial hurdles, over which we must leap before progressing to anything else, and that once vaulted they can be forgotten about. It would seem more accurate to view them as keeping pace with whatever investigative race we run, periodically reminding us of the narrowness of our single lane. Indeed, perhaps they serve a function almost like that of the slaves who walked beside Roman generals and emperors at the head of their triumphal processions, and whispered reminders of their mere mortality, lest they be carried away by the glories of present success.

A third assessment of the likely outcome of Cipher's quest might take its point of departure R. S. Lee's observation, that 'attitudes of belief or unbelief are never reached by processes of reasoning alone',[8] and object that Cipher's intended search for peace of mind in the hall of mirrors infringes the strictures of this truism. After all, 'a correctly reasoned god', as Woods put it, 'is not the object of religious devotion'.[9] Thus Cipher's quest is *fated* to be unsuccessful. Trying to work out a position of religious commitment in a deliberate, rational way is akin to trying to carry water in a net, it is attempting to achieve a goal with a quite unsuitable method. In his autobiography, subtitled 'The Story of My Experiments with Truth', Gandhi records somewhat ruefully how 'it was in England that I first discovered the futility of mere religious knowledge'.[10] And later, in South Africa, he records how Pearson's marvellously entitled book, *Many Infallible Proofs* had, as he put it, 'no effect on me'.[11] Is Cipher not risking an overestimation of the usefulness of 'mere religious knowledge', if he is expecting some sort of infallible proof to emerge from his inquiry and point unambiguously in the direction of his desired commitment? Is this not to misconceive the fundamental nature of human religiousness?

Two points can be raised in reply to such an assessment. The first accepts that a position of commitment *is* very rarely reached by a process of reasoning alone; it is seldom the outcome of a deliberate strategy in which it was viewed as the final goal. Argument is one way of forging towards some sort of certainty, but in the religious realm it is by no means the primary *modus operandi*. As Eliade has remarked, perhaps in a religious context we must

content ourselves with personal certitudes, with wagers based on dreams, with divinations, ecstasies, aesthetic emotions. That is also a mode of knowing, but without arguments.[12]

At the same time as acknowledging the futility of mere religious knowledge, though, we ought to remember that for someone in Cipher's position, a deliberate plan of inquiry is demanded by the unsatisfactoriness of his uncommitted status – regardless of whether or not the outworking of that plan is an *ideal* strategy for the circumstances. Embarking on a quest for peace of mind in the context of the hall of mirrors is, in short, preferable to doing nothing, however inappropriate it may be.

The second point which might be raised in reply to this sort of assessment of Cipher's intended quest, an assessment which sees it as ill-suited to the goal he seeks because religion is not reducible to reason, is to point out that the method he intends using is not strictly discursive. 'Passing over' has been likened to acting rather than, say, to a process of logical reasoning. Moreover, in taking Cipher towards the heart of the matter, it would, if successful, act to take him towards a locus where words and concepts, reason's tools, seem not to work. If Cipher's intended quest is likened to an attempt to penetrate to the '*bindu* point' of a complex *yantra*, i.e. to the empty space at the centre of a complex interlocking mesh of triangles which surround and define it, as this is depicted in the diagrams used in Hinduism and Buddhism to aid meditation, *rather* than as something which focuses on the triangles themselves, then perhaps its approach may not seem as out of keeping with the goal which is being sought.

We could continue with these anticipatory assessments of the result of Cipher's intended quest over a wide area of possible outcomes, but since they *are* all underlain by the necessity to wait and see, to review things after a programme of passing over has been attempted, it would be unsatisfactory to continue for too long on so hypothetical a note.

Regardless of the outcome which might, in fact, be reached after passing over has been attempted, it is, at least, unlikely that Cipher will have to proceed alone. Although I have stressed the dangers of taking him as representative of any large-scale group, it is perhaps worth noting that the conditions necessary for the emergence of such a group seem increasingly to be being established by the way in which the whole area of religion is presented in a school context. For educationalists are intent on providing information across a wide spectrum of faiths; multi-faith religious education is in, mono-faith religious education is out. Whilst in many respects this marks a big improvement from the old indoctrinatory confessionalist approaches, alarmingly little thought seems to have been given to the consequences for individual religiousness which stem from an exposure to the teachings of many faiths.

It is currently fashionable to write handbooks of comparative religion which are, as R. C. Zaehner put it in the preface to one of them,

guidebook(s) to (the) beliefs and religions of the world ... but guidebook(s) in which the editor may not, in the interests of objectivity, assign stars to those religious structures which seem to him the most admirable.[13]

The task of assigning stars is left to the reader himself. Such books are a staple resource of modern religious education at school. But to continue Zaehner's analogy, how much use is a guidebook, if it tells us the history of a country hotel and how those who have stayed in it have viewed the world, but does not tell us that in some rooms the roof leaks?

One off-shoot from a consideration of Cipher's problems – and an important one – is the question of how religious education ought to proceed in a situation of religious plurality. If, after all, as Stanley Samartha would have it, 'religious pluralism, in the last analysis, means that there are fundamentally different answers to the problems of existence',[14] then, indeed, as Edward Hulmes has forcefully argued, religious education is really all about choosing sides.[15] It is about making *decisions*, not just accumulating and understanding information. What the different sides are, how they relate to each other, on what grounds any choice between them ought to be made, when it ought to be made in the course of an individual's development, and how it will affect a person's outlook, remain critically unclear issues which constitute a twilight zone across virtually all the theological, philosophical and psychological aspects involved. In such a twilight zone it is all too easy to stumble towards quite unsound conclusions and adopt highly inappropriate educational policies.

Much of the impetus for such religious education has, of course, stemmed from the disciplinary area of religious studies – that collection of disciplines which have together done so much to facilitate easy access to the hall of mirrors, yet have provided few suggestions about orientation once we are there. Cipher has turned to religious studies on a number of occasions, often with little satisfaction, and doubtless will do so again. But in doing so he is, in many respects, likely to find himself in a position similar to that of the man who turns to philosophy for answers to the great questions about meaning and destiny. As William Barrett has shown, although originally philosophy was concerned with 'the soul's search for salvation',[16] and indeed in an oriental setting is still taken up and practised in order to find such salvation, in a Western context it has become so specialized as to appear to have forgotten its original purpose. Barrett writes:

Specialization is the price we pay for the advancement of knowledge. A price, because the path of specialization leads away from the ordinary and concrete acts of understanding in terms of which man actually lives his day to day life.[17]

In the study of religion too, specialization has led towards an advancement in knowledge. An individual such as Cipher may, however, be left asking whether the price that has been paid is simply too great. Has our knowledge not now, perhaps, advanced far enough to consider a return to beginnings and a focusing on matters of more pressing concern than much of that which it has become accustomed to dealing with? Perhaps he might remind those scholars who are embarrassed by what Barrett calls the 'aboriginal claims',[18] which the non-specialist may still make on their subject, of Collingwood's remark:

If thought were the mere discovery of interesting facts, its indulgence, in a world full of desperate evils and among men crushed beneath the burden of daily tasks too hard for their solitary strength, would be the act of a traitor. . . . We try to understand ourselves and our world only in order that we may learn how to live.[19]

Whether we assess Cipher's intended quest as likely to end up leading him round in circles, bringing him up against a brick wall, or as taking him to some quite different destination, and whether we see him as a solitary figure or one in whose steps many others may tread, we can, I think, quite usefully see the whole drama of commitment in a religiously plural world as taking place in summary in Wisdom's garden.

In Chapter 4, I referred to John Wisdom's by now famous parable which illustrates so well the religiously ambiguous nature of the world. Wisdom imagined a situation where two people return to their long neglected garden, and find among the weeds one or two of the old plants still surprisingly vigorous. One of them decides that a gardener must have been looking after things. The other decides that everything can be explained by chance, that no one has been looking after the garden, and that, given the overgrown state of things, it would be unreasonable to infer that any gardener came.

Wisdom's garden is not just some distant metaphorical territory, staked out with stark precision in the abstract reaches of a philosophical consciousness: we walk through it here and now, and the need to know about its nature, and how we ought to live in it, is a pressing one. To momentarily de-analogize: the garden is the world, more particularly the human situation in that world, and Wisdom's two observers with their theories about the gardener represent theistic and atheistic views. Wisdom's garden, for all its apparent story-time innocuousness, is a testing ground, if not a killing field, for natural theology – if we understand by this term the attempt to look at the world and establish if there are any *definitely* religious cues amidst its perplexing ambiguity – an ambiguity which has led John Bowker to hold that 'faith and despair are equal readings of the natural order'.[20] In an 'unfriendly, friendly universe',[21] to use the poet Edwin Muir's description, in a world where R. W. Hepburn has suggested that 'neither a satanic or a benign vision exhausts nature's ambiguity',[22] *are* there sufficient cues in one direction or the other to allow Cipher to make some sort of world decision, beyond simply accepting the existence of a pervasive ambiguity?

As we have seen, Wisdom's analysis seems to suggest that there are two basic interpretative streams – in some ways rather like William James' notions of the sick-souled and healthy-minded outlooks – whose currents act to draw every phenomenon met with in the garden into their interpretative flow. For Cipher, of course, there are not just two currents of thought, but a veritable interpretative whirlpool in which there are pressures coming from a whole spectrum of different opinions. Are there any features of the garden which would suggest unambiguously that he should navigate his course towards commitment in one particular direction?

Perhaps the best way in which to picture Cipher's situation in the setting of Wisdom's garden is to see him as being aware of the existence there of *many different* vantage points, Hindu, Buddhist, Christian, Jewish, Islamic and so on in all their variety, from which, so those who have ascended their steps claim, the world appears in a particular light. In a sense, at the risk of my menagerie of metaphors running riot and blurring the whole issue, there are vantage points from which, so *some* denizens of the garden say, one can catch a glimpse of some sense-giving salamander. Others claim that these purported vantage points are mere castles in the sky, which look out on a perspective of pure make-believe. Cipher will be concerned, through passing over, to explore the outlooks of those who claim that religions offer an ultimately realistic outlook on life. He will be concerned to ascend the steps of whatever vantage point is offered, and to try to see from there what picture of the world is suggested.

Indeed, given the setting in which Wisdom's metaphor allows us to place him, there is a sense in which we might at this point simply advise Cipher to take a walk in the garden – and to make sure that he chooses some spot where its rural charms are unspoiled, perhaps the more overgrown the better; for Rudolf Otto has warned that the sense of the numinous (which he sees as lying at the core of religiousness) may be sharply affected by surroundings, forest glades being more conducive to it than, say, urban Berlin.[23] Likewise, Ninian Smart has suggested that some city environments can give rise to untypical religious assessments of things.[24] Such ideas about the importance of environment for religious experience are borne out by David Hay, whose book, *Exploring Inner Space*, was referred to at some length in Chapter 3. Hay notes that 'the larger the city is, the less frequently is religious experience reported in it',[25] and he concludes that perhaps 'the absence of religious experience could be like every other impoverishment, an alienation of people's natural powers'.[26]

In Aldous Huxley's *Brave New World*, the savage, an individual who lives outside the luxuries and comforts of this apparent utopia, remarks: 'It is natural to believe in God when you're alone – quite alone, in the night, thinking about death.'[27] To which the swift rejoinder from the establishment is: 'People in our society never *are* alone, and we try to ensure that their thoughts do not turn in this particular direction'. One begins to wonder if there may not, perhaps, be a sense in which Cipher's return to beginnings should take him in the direction of a period of solitary meditation in a natural wilderness, where he may re-familiarize himself with the basic conditions of the *same house*, of the human situation, rather than focusing his attention exclusively on interpretations of it. Wisdom's suggestion of a garden as the arena in which the religious debate occurs is, perhaps, appropriate in a sense he did not intend.

*   *   *

I must confess that it was my original intention to entitle this final chapter, 'Lessons from Three Elephants', but, looking back over my other titles, I got cold feet in the end, and thought that something less peculiar might provide a welcome balance for those readers whose patience has already been sorely tried by slaps, salamanders, skulls on mantels and other such devices. But even though they may not feature directly in the title, I'm afraid I am going to use these theologically unlikely beasts to stress some simple but important points which Cipher must bear in mind and carry forward to the next stage of his inquiry.

The first elephant is brought on by the question: 'can those who have examined such a creature only through a microscope claim to understand it properly?' One reply is, of course, to toss the query back and ask if those who relied solely on the unaided naked eye could claim any greatly superior understanding. Indeed, many morals could be drawn from this question and the replies which can be made to it. The lesson for Cipher, though, is quite straightforward: it is more important for him to deal with the naked-eye perspective on religion before reaching for his microscope. This is to re-emphasize the point, that the urgency of his quest should not allow itself to be side-tracked or submerged beneath the intricacies of a descriptive, phenomenological approach. If the focus is to be be kept on *making a decision about commitment* then Cipher must remember, going back to the passage about Sherlock Holmes which was quoted in Chapter 2, that much of what occurs on the microscopic level — although of considerable interest to scholars — will not make 'a pennyworth of difference' to his quest for peace of mind. Although a naked-eye perspective may be accused of being too simple, or even superficial, its range of concerns seems far more appropriate to Cipher's situation in the religious hall of mirrors than those which would be raised by a microscopic focus.

The second elephant is introduced by an ancient Eastern story which has become quite well known in the West, particularly in theological circles, where it has percolated through one wonders what channels of inter-cultural communication to appear in the writings of Hans Küng and John Hick.[28] It is the story about the three blind men who are given the task of finding out what an elephant is like. On reporting back their various tactile sensations – for, improbably, the elephant let them touch it – one says, 'It's like a snake'; the second, that 'it's like a wall'; and the third, that 'it's like a tree-trunk'. Their reports, which, incidentally, illustrate the importance of comparison in apprehending something new, differ so greatly, because one had caught hold of the elephant's tail, the other had placed his hands on its side, and the third had grasped one of its legs.

One lesson which might be drawn from such a story is that any attempt which approximates to a survey of the religions of the world undertaken with the intention of establishing which one is best, may be wholly misguided in what it is trying to do. This kind of simplistic, competition-type approach, in which a champion is thought to have emerged after all other competitors have been bludgeoned from the ring by a sustained critical onslaught, is, one hopes, a dying sport anyway; but reminders of its inappropriateness are useful, nonetheless, given that Cipher is concerned with evaluation in a religiously plural context. As we see an increasing number of points of similarity between them, the idea of making Hinduism, Buddhism, Judaism, Christianity, Islam and so on into sparring partners, let alone competitors in some sort of fight to the death, seems more and more inappropriate. Such an exercise might well be placing too much faith in blind men's reports, assuming that there are several different elephants rather than a single beast. As it would be a bizarre endeavour to try to select which part of the elephant in the story was 'best', so too it might be similarly misguided to try to elevate any single religious tradition to a position of victorious pre-eminence. Of course, as John Hick points out, the parable of the blind men and the elephant is only effective in conveying a warning in this way, if we are in a position to see the whole elephant and realize that it is, in fact, a single beast – precisely the perspective which is lacking when it comes to our view of religions. So, any lesson drawn from the story must be a tentative and provisional one. Indeed we could, perhaps, with Hick's comment in mind, also use the story as a warning against swallowing metaphors hook, line and sinker.

The third and final elephant is the one which occurs in
Haribhadra's famous story of Samaraditya, an ancient Jain
parable (though Hindu versions are also known) which has
reached the Western consciousness largely via Tolstoy's *Con-
fessions*, and William James' extensive citing of Tolstoy in
The Varieties of Religious Experience.[29] The story tells of a
man wandering lost in a forest. Suddenly a mad elephant
appears out of nowhere and charges him. He flees in terror
towards a huge banyan tree, but finds to his dismay that there
are no branches near enough the ground to allow him to climb
up to safety. At the foot of the tree, though, there is an old
well, and in desperation the man jumps into it. As he falls he
reaches out and grabs hold of a clump of vegetation growing
from the side of the well. As he clings to it he begins to take in
his new surroundings, whilst above, the mad elephant charges
against the tree. Looking below he sees that the well is
occupied by a giant serpent, which needs only to wait for him
to fall, for two mice – one white, the other black – are
gnawing in turn at the stem of the plant to which he hangs.
Eventually the elephant's charging dislodges a bees' nest from
the overhanging branches of the tree. The nest falls into the
well and the man is badly stung. However, some drops of
honey trickle into his mouth and its taste of sweetness allows
him, momentarily, to forget about the perils which surround
him on all sides.

The story is dense with imagery and I have given a considerably simplified version. It can be read in many different
ways: some see it simply as an illustration of the inevitable
and unavoidable nature of pain and death, others of the way
in which pleasure can cloud our vision – either mercifully or
fatally, depending on whether there is any possibility of
escape.

One interpretation which could be offered casts both
elephant and serpent as personifications of death, which no
one can avoid indefinitely, whilst the banyan tree represents
the salvific potentiality offered by religion, representing peace
of mind and ultimate security. The white mouse symbolizes
day, the black one night, and together, as the flow of time,
they eat their way through every individual's life-span. The
story is a powerful statement of *the massive religious sense of*

something wrong with the world, to which attention was drawn earlier. It sees the fundamental elements of the *same house*, of the human situation, as something desperately in need of a curative, sense-giving, security-offering response, *not* as something which is self-sufficient in terms of meaning. To accommodate Cipher's situation of perceived religious plurality, we would have to imagine that the well was ringed with many different trees, not just overhung by a single banyan. The dilemma he faces involves deciding which, if any, offers legitimate security. Commitment would involve the difficult and strenuous process of clambering out of the well and into its branches.

At the end of the day, the most fundamental question which Cipher will have to decide on is a twofold one: *first*, whether to accept as accurate a religious diagnosis of the precarious and unpleasant position involved in the religiously unaided human situation, and *secondly*, whether there is, in fact, a genuine possibility of salvation from it. The question of choice, set amidst a variety of purported salvific resources, is very much secondary to deciding if such resources are necessary in the first place. If he rejects either the basic religious diagnosis of something wrong with the world, in the sense of its needing reference to some kind of transcendent state or entity to ensure peace of mind, or if he rejects the possibility of there being any peace of mind in this sense, then the chances are that he will concentrate on enjoying as much honey as he can for as long as possible. If he accepts a religious reading of the human situation, seeing it as futile unless reference is made to some sense-giving transcendent entity or state such as God or Nirvana, and if he accepts that such expressions of transcendence which claim to bring the human situation into meaningful focus are more than just illusions, he might, perhaps, conclude that the well is a precarious place from which to conduct his inquiries. Maybe his first task is to get to the safety of tree-level, from where he may then start to look around. Such a strategy, which might usefully have been commended to Buridan's ass, would, of course, risk ascending in the wrong direction, but perhaps that is a lesser gamble than remaining uncommitted for too long.

Notes

Full bibliographical details are only given when a work is cited for the first time; they are not repeated thereafter. Dates in brackets indicate date of first publication, where this differs from the publication date of the edition used.

Chapter One

1. Flann O'Brien, *At Swim Two Birds*, London, 1966 (1939), Hart-Davis, MacGibbon Ltd., p. 54.
2. ibid., p. 57
3. ibid., p. 59.
4. ibid.
5. David Hume, *An Enquiry Concerning Human Understanding*, Oxford, 1894, (1748), Oxford University Press, Selby-Bigge edition, Section 4 Part 1 p. 28.
6. ibid., Section 5 Part 1 p. 44.
7. In choosing to call my imaginary character 'Cipher' I do not want to bring to mind, beyond noting its occurrence and possible future relevance, the concept of the same name which plays so fundamental a part in Karl Jaspers' philosophy. Since for Jaspers the centrally important cipher of 'foundering' 'signifies the fruitlessness of all endeavours to reach, from a finite basis ... a satisfactory access to Being, i.e., to arrive at the absolute', the *character* Cipher might, eventually, in some future philosophical stage of his search, consider whether or not what he is attempting falls under such a condemnation. However, for the purposes of that part of his search which will be dealt with in this book, Cipher and his readers can simply lay to one side as accidental any implications which may be read off Jaspers' remarks on 'ciphers' or 'cipher-script'. That my choice of 'Cipher' as a name for the heuristic fiction herein created, occurred long before my learning of Jaspers' use of the term, underlines the coincidental nature of the identical nomenclature

and warns against assuming any great significance in its occurrence in two such totally different contexts. On Jaspers' concept of foundering, see Johannes Thyssen, 'The Concept of "Foundering" in Jaspers' Philosophy', pp. 297–235 in Paul Arthur Schilpp (ed.), *The Philosophy of Karl Jaspers*, New York, 1957, Tudor Publishing Co. The quotation above is taken from p. 312 of Thyssen's article.

8. See Martin Hollis, *Models of Man*, Philosophical Thoughts on Social Action, Cambridge, 1977, Cambridge University Press, pp. 20–21.

9. George Steiner, *Language and Silence*, Essays 1958–1966, London, 1985, (1967), Faber, pp. 180–181.

10. Virginia Woolf, *Jacob's Room*, Harmondsworth, 1971, (1922), Penguin, p. 90.

11. Thucydides, *The Peloponnesian War*, Book 2 Chapter 5.

12. Ninian Smart, *Beyond Ideology*, Religion and the Future of Western Civilization, London, 1981, (the Gifford Lectures at the University of Edinburgh, 1979–1980), Collins, p. 21.

13. Peter L. Berger, *The Heretical Imperative*, Contemporary Possibilities of Religious Affirmation, London, 1980, (1979), Collins, p. 11.

14. ibid.

15. George Rupp, *Beyond Existentialism and Zen*, Religion in a Pluralistic World, New York, 1979, Oxford University Press, p. 10.

16. Hendrick Kraemer, *Religion and the Christian Faith*, London, 1956, Lutterworth Press, p. 22.

17. Flann O'Brien, op. cit., p. 55.

18. P. D. James, *Death of an Expert Witness*, London, 1983 (1977), Sphere Books, p. 186.

19. Douglas Adams, *The Hitch Hiker's Guide to the Galaxy*, London 1979, Pan Books, p. 135f.

20. Karl Britton, *Philosophy and the Meaning of Life*, Cambridge, 1969, Cambridge University Press, p. 12.

21. The Dalai Lama, *My Land and My People*, the Autobiography of His Holiness the Dalai Lama, edited by David Howarth, London, 1962, Weidenfeld & Nicholson, p. 211.

22. Robert Pirsig, *Zen and the Art of Motorcycle Maintenance*, London, 1974, The Bodley Head.

23. Max Black, *Models and Metaphors*, Studies in Language and Philosophy, New York, 1962, Cornell University Press, p. 237. I hope further to explore the methodological potential which metaphor has for the study of religion in my forthcoming second

series of Gifford Research Fellowship Lectures, 'Waking from Sleep as a Metaphor for the Religious Dynamic'.

24. William Beveridge, *Private Thoughts Upon Religion*, Glasgow, 1753, (1709), William Duncan Junior, p. 9.
25. ibid.
26. Wilfred Cantwell Smith, *The Meaning and End of Religion*, London, 1978, (1962), SPCK, p. 2.
27. ibid.
28. ibid.
29. Wilfred Cantwell Smith, *Questions of Religious Truth*, London, 1967, Gollancz, p. 35.
30. ibid.
31. The problems posed by religious plurality for Christian commitment have received extensive treatment. Among the more recent volumes which Cipher's Christian first-cousins might look to for advice are: Stephen Neill, *The Christian Faith and Other Faiths*, The Christian Dialogue with Other Religions, London, 1970, 2nd edition (1961), Oxford University Press; A. K. Cragg, *The Christian and Other Religion*, London, 1977, Mowbray; Alan Race, *Christians and Religious Pluralism*, Patterns in Christian Theology of Religions, London, 1983, SCM; Paul Knitter, *No Other Name?* A Critical Study of Christian Attitudes Towards the World Religions, London 1985, SCM; Gavin D'Costa, *Theology and Religious Pluralism*, The Challenge of Other Religions, Oxford 1986, Basil Blackwell.
32. Wilfred Cantwell Smith, *The Meaning and End of Religion*, p. 12.
33. ibid., p. 50.
34. ibid., p. 60.
35. Wilfred Cantwell Smith, *Questions of Religious Truth*, p. 107.
36. Wilfred Cantwell Smith, *The Meaning and End of Religion*, p. 7.
37. Ludwig Wittgenstein, *Notebooks 1914–1916*, Oxford, 1961, Basil Blackwell, edited by G. H. Von Wright and G. E. M. Anscombe, translated by G. E. M. Anscombe, pp. 72–73e.

Chapter Two

1. Brihadaranyaka Upanishad, 1.3.28. Translation from Shree Purohit Swami and W. B. Yeats (trs.) *The Ten Principal Upanishads*, London, 1971, (1937), Faber, p. 119.

2. Pietro Rossano, 'Christ's Lordship and Religious Pluralism in Roman Catholic Perspective', in Gerald H. Anderson and Thomas F. Stransky (eds.) *Christ's Lordship and Religious Pluralism*, New York, 1981, Orbis Books, p. 98.

3. Edith B. Schnapper, *The Inward Odyssey*, the Concept of The Way in the Great Religions of the World, London, 1980, (1965), George Allen & Unwin, p. 86.

4. Romans 7.19.

5. David Gnanaprakasam Moses, *Religious Truth and the Relation Between Religions*, Madras, 1950, The Christian Literature Society for India, Indian Research Series 5, pp. 91–92.

6. Aldous Huxley, *Eyeless in Gaza*, Harmondsworth, 1974 (1936), Penguin, p. 12.

7. Quoted in Mircea Eliade, *From Primitives to zen*, A Thematic Sourcebook of the History of Religions, London, 1979, (1967), Collins, p. 326.

8. Arnold Toynbee, *Mankind and Mother Earth*, London, 1976, Oxford University Press, p. 4.

9. Mircea Eliade, *A History of Religious Ideas*, Vol. 1: From the Stone Age to the Eleusinian Mysteries, London, 1979, (1976), Collins, p. xiii.

10. Mircea Eliade, *No Souvenirs*, Journal 1957–1969, London, 1978, (1973), Routledge & Kegan Paul, p. viii.

11. See René Descartes, *Philosophical Works*, Vol. 1, Cambridge, 1973, (this edition 1911), Cambridge University Press, tr. Haldane and Ross, p. 82.

12. Quoted in Partha Mitter, *Much Maligned Monsters*, A History of European Reactions to Indian Art, Oxford, 1977, Clarendon Press, p. 20.

13. ibid.

14. P. J. Marshall (ed.), *The British Discovery of Hinduism in the Eighteenth Century*, Cambridge, 1970, Cambridge University Press, p. 20.

15. ibid., p. 43.

16. Max Müller, *Chips From a German Workshop*, Vol. 1: Essays on the Science of Religion, London, 1867, p. xxx.

17. James C. Moffat, *A Comparative History of Religions*, New York, 1875, Dodd & Mead, Vol. 1, p. vi.

18. Emile Burnouf, *The Science of Religions*, London, 1888, (1870), Swan, Sonnenschein, Lowrey & Co., p. 1.

19. Ralph Wendell Burhoe, 'The Phenomenon of Religion seen Scientifically', in Allan W. Eister (ed.), *Changing Perspectives in the Scientific study of Religion*, New York, 1974, Wiley Inter-

science, p. 15. Burhoe's opinion echoes that of Edwin Starbuck, voiced some seventy five years earlier in his *Psychology of Religion*, London, 1899, who contrasts the study of religion with the history of science and concludes that 'the study of religion is today where astronomy and chemistry were four centuries ago' (p. 3). Alister Hardy would, apparently, disagree with this assessment of the situation, suggesting that in William James and in Starbuck himself we already have parallels, in what he calls 'the biology of God', to Darwin and Wallace in (non-theistic) biology. See *The Biology of God*, a Scientist's Study of Man the Religious Animal, London, 1975, Cape, p. 20.

20. Georg Schmid, *Principals of Integral Science of Religion*, The Hague, 1979, Mouton, p. 5.

21. Louis Henry Jordan, *Comparative Religion, its Genesis and Growth*, Edinburgh, 1905, T & T Clark, p. 163.

22. G. F. Woods, *Theological Explanations*, A Study of the Meaning and Means of Explaining in Science, History and Theology, Welwyn, 1958, James Nisbet & Co. Ltd., p. 2.

23. Eric J. Sharpe, *Comparative Religion*, A History, London, 1975, Duckworth, p. 2.

24. Georg Schmid, op. cit, p. 19.

25. C. J. Bleeker, *The Sacred Bridge*, Researches into the Nature and Structure of Religion, Leiden 1963, E. J. Brill, p. 11.

26. See Frederick J. Streng, 'Religious Studies: Process of Transformation', in *The Proceedings of the American Academy of Religion*, Academic Study of Religion Section, 1974, p. 118. The sociological difficulties in holding to a single belief system in a situation of religious plurality, have been clearly spelt out by Peter Berger in *A Rumour of Angels*, Modern Society and the Rediscovery of the Supernatural, Harmondsworth, 1970, (1969), Penguin, pp. 61–62, where he writes: 'The pluralistic situation not only allows the individual a choice, it forces him to choose. By the same token, it makes religious certainty very hard to come by' (p. 62).

27. Arthur Miles (pseudonym of Gervee Baronté), *The Land of the Lingam*, London, 1933, Paternoster Press, pp. 7 and 9.

28. Ernest Becker, *The Denial of Death*, New York, 1973 The Free Press, p.x.

29. Georg Schmid, op. cit., p. 18.

30. Arthur Conan Doyle, *A Study in Scarlet*, Harmondsworth, 1981, (1887), Penguin, reprinted in *The Penguin Complete Sherlock Holmes*, p. 21.

Chapter Three

1. Peter Berger, *A Rumour of Angels*, Modern Society and the Rediscovery of the Supernatural, Harmondsworth, 1971, (1969), Penguin, p. 18f.
2. Leszek Kolakowski, *Religion*, If There is no God. . . . On God, the Devil, Sin and other worries of the so called Philosophy of Religion, Glasgow, 1982, Fontana Books, p. 12.
3. Henri-Frédéric Amiel, journal entry dated 17th December 1856. See *Amiel's Journal, the Journal Intime of Henri-Frédéric Amiel*, tr. with an introduction and notes by Mrs Humphrey Ward, London, 1913, (1885), Macmillan.
4. R. C. Zaehner, *The City Within the Heart*, London, 1980, Unwin, p. 6.
5. David Hay, *Exploring Inner Space*, Scientists and Religious Experience, Harmondsworth, 1982, Penguin, p. 28.
6. J. C. A. Gaskin, *The Quest for Eternity*, An Outline of the Philosophy of Religion, Harmondsworth, 1984, Penguin, p. 174. My emphasis.
7. David Hay, op. cit., p. 55.
8. ibid., p. 69.
9. ibid.
10. ibid., p. 118.
11. ibid., p. 212.
12. Daishin Morgan, 'Choosing Your Way', *The Journal of Throssel Hole Priory*, Vol. X no. 1, Spring 1983, p. 7.
13. Willard Gurdun Oxtoby, 'Religionswissenschaft Revisited', in Jacob Neusner (ed.), *Religions in Antiquity*, Essays in Memory of Erwin Ramsdell Goodenough, Leiden, 1968, E. J. Brill, p. 596.
14. Joachim Wach, *Sociology of Religion*, London, 1947, Kegan Paul, Trench, Trubner & Co. Ltd (in the International Library of Sociology and Social Reconstruction series, edited by Karl Mannheim), p. 14. Although Wach voices agreement with MacMurray in terms of the way in which the modern study of religion focuses on response rather than stimulus (citing the latter's *The Structure of Religious Experience*, London, 1936, Faber, pp. 20 and 43), he would not characterize the stimulus in the same way.
15. Benvenuto Cellini, *Autobiography*, New York, undated, Random House Modern Library, tr. by John Addington Symonds, p. 9 (1728).

16. 'To designate the *act of manifestation* of the sacred, we have proposed the term *hierophany*. It is a fitting term, because it does not imply anything further; it expresses no more than is implicated in its etymological content, i.e. *that something sacred shows itself to us*'. Mircea Eliade, *The Sacred and Profane*, the Nature of Religion, New York, 1959, (1957), Harcourt Brace & World, p. 11. Many varieties of hierophany are mapped out in detail in Eliade's classic study, *Patterns in Comparative Religion*, London, 1976, (1958), Sheed & Ward, where we find hierophany described as 'a manifestation of the sacred in the mental world of those who believed in it' (p. 10). Whether or not any particular hierophany does in fact stem from some transcendent state or entity separate from and independent of the mental world of the individual who believes it to come from, say, a certain deity, remains one of Cipher's key questions.

17. Lesslie Newbigin, 'Teaching Religion in a Secular Plural Society', in John Hull (ed.), *New Directions in Religious Education*, Lewes, 1982, Falmer Press, p. 105.

18. ibid.

19. These various ways of characterizing an approach emphasizing 'stimulus' or 'response' are taken from the vocabularies of Wilfred Cantwell Smith (the terms 'personal faith' and 'cumulative tradition' are introduced in his *The Meaning and End of Religion*, see especially Chapters 6 and 7); Ninian Smart (the terms 'parahistorical' and 'historical' are introduced in his *Secular Education and the Logic of Religions*, London, 1968, Faber, see especially Chapter 1); and Georg Schmid (the terms 'the reality of religion' and 'religious reality' are introduced in his *Principles of Integral Science of Religion*, see especially p. 10f.). It would obviously be difficult, if not impossible (and it would certainly be distorting) to emphasize one element in any of these pairs to the total exclusion of the other. A stimulus would be invisible without some response and a response considered without reference to its stimulus would be meaningless.

20. J. C. A. Gaskin, op. cit., p. 16f.

21. Michael Novak, *Ascent of the Mountain, Flight of the Dove*, An Invitation to Religious Studies, New York, 1978, (1971), Harper & Row, p. xvii.

Chapter Four

1. Quoted in Nirad C. Chaudhuri, *Scholar Extraordinary*, the Life of Professor the Right Honourable Friedrich Max Müller, PC, London, 1974, Chatto & Windus, p. 345.
2. Wilfred Cantwell Smith, *The Faith of Other Men*, New York, 1972, (1963), Harper & Row, p. 11.
3. ibid., p. 132.
4. Langdon Gilkey, 'God', in Peter Hodgson and Robert King (eds.), *Christian Theology*, An Introduction to its Traditions and Tasks, London, 1983, (1982), SPCK, p. 85.
5. ibid., p. 86. My emphasis.
6. John Hick, *God and the Universe of Faiths*, London, 1977, (1973), Collins, p. 131.
7. This passage, from *Euripides and his Age*, inspires the title and provides the epigraph for the report from which I take it, *Heirs and Rebels*, Principles and Practicalities in Christian Education, Blandford, 1982, issued by the Bloxham Project, Chairman: Basil Mitchell.
8. Thomas Mann, *Dr. Faustus*, Harmondsworth, 1973, (1947), Penguin, p. 406.
9. Max Müller, *Thoughts on Life and Religion*, An Aftermath from the Writings of Max Müller by his Wife, London, 1906, (1905), Archibald Constable & Co., pp. 101 and 235.
10. Eugene Marais, *The Soul of the White Ant*, Harmondsworth, 1973, (1937), Penguin, p. 78.
11. Huston Smith, *The Religions of Man*, New York, 1958, Harper & Row, p. 230.
12. ibid., p. 4.
13. See William James, *The Varieties of Religious Experience*, A Study in Human Nature, (The Gifford Lectures in Edinburgh for 1901–02), Lectures 4–7.
14. John Wisdom, 'Gods', *Proceedings of the Aristotelian Society*, 1944–1945, p. 185f. Whilst Marais and Müller fall easily into James' sick souled and healthy minded categories, applying them without careful qualification to the characters in Wisdom's tale would be unwise.
15. Laurence Sterne, *The Life and Opinions of Trisram Shandy*, London, 1950, (1760), Rupert Hart Davis, edited by J. A. Work, p. 151.
16. See Chapter 1 note 13.
17. See Antony Flew's contribution to the 'Theology and

Falsification' debate in *New Essays in Philosophical Theology*, London, 1969, (1955), SCM, especially p. 99.

18. I am using this phrase in a simplified sense. I do not intend its appearance in Cipher's methodological vocabulary to endorse as appropriate to his particular situation the programme and procedures followed in Dunne's passing over trilogy – *The City of the Gods* (1965), a passing over to cultures; *A Search for God in Time and Memory* (1967), a passing over to lives; and *The Way of All the Earth* (1972), a passing over to religions. In the last mentioned volume, Dunne describes passing over as 'a method of entering sympathetically into another person's autobiographical standpoint, seeing the whole world anew as that person sees it'; it involves the attempt 'to enter sympathetically into the feelings of another person, become receptive to the images which give expression to his feelings (and) attain insight into those images' (p. 53). It is in this straightforward sense of providing a technique for closely observing outlooks on the world other than one's own that I am using the term 'passing over' here. Whether or not such passing over will provide sufficient insight to 'guide one into the future' and provide 'a new understanding of one's life', as Dunne suggests (ibid.), must, from Cipher's point of view, remain to be seen. Although, in the preface to *A Search for God in Time and Memory*, Dunne asserts unequivocally that 'the method of passing over is the one I will be using in this book' (p. ix) and, in fact (as remarked above), describes his three books in terms of their being a methodological trilogy applying this technique to different areas (see *The Way of All the Earth* pp. ix–x), it is not always easy to connect the few explicit details given about passing over with the full range of its (apparent) application. Nevertheless, whatever criticisms might be voiced, it is clear that these three volumes should find a place on Cipher's bookshelf. (British editions are published in London by Sheldon Press). Passing over has, perhaps, some interesting points of comparison with Henri-Frédéric Amiel's concept of 'reimplication'. On this see Herbert Spiegelberg, 'Amiel's "New Phenomenology"', *Archiv für Geschichte Der Philosophie*, Vol. 49 (1967) pp. 201–214, especially p. 212. A further point of clarifying comparison might be with R. G. Collingwood's concept of doing history where the historian is called upon to 're-enact the past in his own mind'. See R. G. Collingwood, *The Idea of History*, Oxford, 1970, (1946), Oxford University Press, p. 282.

19. Winston L. King, 'The Phenomenology of Religion', *The Drew Gateway*, Vol. 43 (1972), p. 33.

20. Ninian Smart, *The Science of Religion and the Sociology of Knowledge*, Princeton, 1973, Princeton University Press, p. 20.
21. Gerardus van der Leeuw, 'Confession Scientifique', quoted in translation in Eric J. Sharpe, *Comparative Religion*, A History, London, 1975, Duckworth, p. 231.
22. Rudolf Otto, *The Idea of the Holy*, an Inquiry into the non-Rational Factor in the Idea of the Divine and its Relation to the Rational, Oxford, 1977, (1917) Oxford University Press, tr. John W. Harvey, p. 62.
23. Thus in a letter to Otto dated 5th March 1919, Edmund Husserl wrote, 'Your book on the holy has affected me more powerfully than scarcely any book in years. . . . It is a first beginning for a phenomenology of religiousness. . . .' Quoted in Charles Courtney, 'Phenomenology and Ninian Smart's Philosophy of Religion', *International Journal for Philosophy of Religion*, vol. 9 (1978), p. 48.
24. James Haughton Woods, *The Value of Religious Facts*, A Study of Some Aspects of the Science of Religion, New York, 1899, Dutton, pp. 13–14. See also p. 52f of Woods' *Practice and Science of Religion*, a Study of Method in Comparative Religion, London, 1906, Longmans, Green & Co., where he discusses 'reconstructing the inner meaning' of religious beliefs.
25. Wilfred Cantwell Smith, *The Meaning and End of Religion*, p. 188.
26. ibid.
27. G. K. Chesterton, *The Secret of Father Brown*, Harmondsworth, 1982, (1927), Penguin, *The Penguin Complete Father Brown*, p. 464.
28. ibid. p. 465.
29. ibid.
30. ibid., p. 465–466.
31. William Golding, *A Moving Target*, London, 1982, Faber, p. 104.
32. Walt Whitman, 'Song of Myself', see in particular lines 832–834 and 1096–1108.
33. E. E. Evans-Pritchard, *Theories of Primitive Religion*, Oxford, 1970, (1965), Oxford University Press, pp. 43 & 47.
34. Smart's analogy with acting, mentioned in *The Science of Religion and the Sociology of Knowledge*, receives further attention in his *The Phenomenon of Religion*, New York, 1973, Herder & Herder, p. 75f.
35. Mircea Eliade, *The Forbidden Forest*, Indiana, 1978, (1955), University of Notre Dame Press, tr. Mac Linscott Ricketts and Mary Park Stevenson, p. 192.

Chapter Five

1. Henri-Frédéric Amiel, journal entry dated 26th November 1861. See *Amiel's Journal, the Journal Intime of Henri-Frédéric Amiel*, London, 1913, (1885), Macmillan, tr. Mrs Humphrey Ward. It is interesting to note that James Haughton Woods also views drama in terms of reconstruction. In the course of advocating some such technique in the study of religion, he points to this parallel area in which we are more accustomed to its use: 'This reconstruction of another's will is a familiar process to us. Every drama we have read is an experiment of this kind'. *Practice and Science of Religion*, A Study of Method in Comparative Religion, London, 1906, Longmans, Green & Co., p. 54.

2. Edward W. Said, *Beginnings*, Intention and Method, New York, 1975, Basic Books, pp. 49–50. My emphasis.

3. Chandogya Upanishad 6.1–3 and 12–14, translation taken from Wm. Theodore de Bary (ed.) *Sources of Indian Tradition*, New York, 1970, (1958), Columbia University Press, Vol. 1 p. 33.

4. Georg Schmid, *Principles of the Integral Science of Religion*, pp. 33, 34 and 35.

5. R. Gordon Milburn, *The Religious Mysticism of the Upanishads*, London, 1924, Theosophical Publishing House, p. 7.

6. H. D. Lewis and R. L. Slater, *World Religions*, London, 1966, Watts & Co., p. 143.

7. Rudolf Otto, *The Idea of the Holy*, p. 6.

8. Raimundo Panikkar, *The Intra Religious Dialogue*, New York, 1978, Paulist Press, p. 43.

9. Rudolf Otto, op. cit., pp. 63–64.

10. ibid., p. 77.

11. R. C. Zaehner, *Hinduism*, Oxford, 1977, (1962), Oxford University Press, p. 33.

12. J. D. J. Waardenburg, 'Research on Meaning in Religion', in *Religion, Culture and Methodology* ed. Th.P. van Baaren and H. J. W. Drijvers, The Hague, 1973, Mouton, p. 122.

13. David R. Kinsley, *The Sword and the Flute*, Kali and Krishna, Dark Visions of the Terrible and the Sublime in Hindu Mythology, Berkeley, 1975, University of California Press, p. 6.

14. ibid.

15. ibid., p. 159.

16. W. Brede Kristensen, *The Meaning of Religion*, Lectures in the Phenomenology of Religion, The Hague, 1960, Mouton, p. 7. I have substituted 'Muslims' for the 'Mohammedans' given in the translation.

17. Examples of how coming close to the apparent transcendent reality perceived within an 'alien' tradition may in fact enrich an *existing* religiousness, may be found in Robert A. McDermott, 'Religion as an Academic Discipline', in *Cross Currents*, Vol. 18 (1968) pp. 11–33 (see especially p. 29); and in Harvey Cox, *Turning East*, the Promise and Peril of the New Orientalism, London, 1979, (1977), Allen Lane/Penguin.

18. Edward Farley, *Ecclesial Man*, a Social Phenomenology of Faith and Reality, Philadelphia, 1975, Fortress Press, p. 23.

19. Rudolf Otto has called for 'penetrative imaginative sympathy with what passes in the other person's mind' (*The Idea of the Holy*, p. 62), whilst Ninian Smart has called on the student of religions to 'penetrate into the hearts and minds' of the believers (*The Religious Experience of Mankind*, London, 1973, (1969), Fontana, p. 13).

20. Frederick J. Streng, *Emptiness, a Study in Religious Meaning*, New York, 1967, Abingdon, p. 24.

21. Winston L. King, 'Negation as a Religious Category', *Journal of Religion*, Vol. 37 (1957), p. 108.

22. Paul van Buren, *The Edges of Language*, London, 1972, SCM, p. 157.

23. Quoted in Winston L. King's 'Negation as a Religious Category', p. 107.

24. Qur'an, Chapter 112, Sale's translation, London, no date, Frederick Warne & Co., p. 595. Sale notes that 'this chapter is held in particular veneration by the Mohammedans, and declared, by a tradition of their prophet, to be equal in value to a third part of the whole Koran. It is said to have been revealed in answer to the Koreish, who asked Mohammed concerning the distinguishing attributes of the God he invited them to worship' (ibid.).

25. Quoted in Aldous Huxley, *The Perennial Philosophy*, London, 1950, (1946), Chatto & Windus, p. 32. The scripture to which Shankara refers in Taittirya Upanishad, 2.4.

26. Ninian Smart, *A Dialogue of Religions*, London, 1960, SCM, p. 11.

27. Karl Barth, *Church Dogmatics*, Edinburgh, 1957, T & T Clark, Vol. 2 p. 449. Authorized English translation by T. H. L. Parker, W. B. Johnston, Harold Knight and J. L. M. Haire of *Die Kirchliche Dogmatik II: Die Lehre von Gott*.

28. I. T. Ramsey, *Models and Mystery*, London, 1964, Oxford University Press, p. 60.
29. ibid.
30. J. L. Austin, *Sense and Sensibilia*, Oxford, 1970 (1962), Clarendon Press, p. 74.
31. ibid.
32. W. T. Stace, *Mysticism and Philosophy*, London, 1960, Macmillan, p. 291.
33. John Bowker, *The Religious Imagination and the Sense of God*, Oxford, 1978, Oxford University Press, p. 28.
34. ibid.
35. *Bhagavad Gita*, 6.25, Juan Mascaro's translation, Harmondsworth, 1962, Penguin Classics.

Chapter Six

1. Thornton Wilder, *The Eighth Day*, London, 1967, Longmans, Green & Co., p. 167.
2. Huston Smith, *The Purposes of Higher Education*, New York, 1955, Harper & Row, pp. 36–37.
3. William A. Christian, *Oppositions of Religious Doctrines*, a Study of the Logic of Dialogue among Religions, London, 1972, Macmillan, p. 31.
4. John Bowker, *The Sense of God*, Oxford, 1973, Oxford University Press, p. 13.
5. Morris Jastrow, *The Study of Religion*, London, 1901, Contemporary Science Series, p. 1.
6. see Lauri Honko (ed.), *Science of Religion: Studies in Methodology*, The Hague, 1979, Mouton. This volume consists of the proceedings of the study conference of the International Association for the History of Religions held in Turku, Finland, in 1973.
7. Basil Mitchell, *Neutrality and Commitment*, Oxford, 1968, Clarendon Press, p. 22. This booklet is the text of an inaugural lecture delivered before the University of Oxford in May 1968.
8. Anders Nygren, *Meaning and Method*, Prolegomena to a Scientific Philosophy of Religion and a Scientific Theology, London, 1972, Epworth Press, authorized translation by Philip S. Watson, p. 187.
9. ibid.
10. Jay J. Kim, 'Belief or Anamnesis: is a Rapprochement between History of Religions and Theology Possible?', *Journal of Religion*, Vol. 37. (1957), p. 165.

11. Wilfred Cantwell Smith, *The Meaning and End of Religion*, p. 200.
12. ibid., p. 131.
13. Bernard E. Meland, 'Theology and the Historians of Religion', *Journal of Religion*, Vol. 41 (1961), p. 271.
14. ibid. To further stress that, in the figure of Cipher, I am not advocating as plausible some sort of complete neutrality where an individual approaches religion in a wholly detached and inhumanly objective way, let me endorse Harvey Cox's peculiarly apt remark which emphasizes the common human interest in questions of life and death and underlines how unsatisfactory it would be to remain in a state of permanent indecision about religious commitment: 'The people who study religion are not ciphers. They are faced with the same questions of life and death and right and wrong with which the various religions deal. They cannot avoid the question of truth forever. Economists who investigate rival theories of savings and inflation must decide how to invest their own money. Students of comparative religion eventually have to decide how they are going to live their lives and make their decisions. They have to ask what faith, if any, will guide their ultimate choices. This unavoidable need to choose has pushed the academic study of religion toward a frank acknowledgment that no one can study religion merely descriptively. This in turn makes the modern myths of neutrality and objectivity increasingly implausible.' (*Religion in the Secular City*, New York, 1984, Simon & Schuster, p. 224). I am indebted to Professor Colin Grant, Department of Religious Studies, Mount Allison University, New Brunswick, Canada, for drawing my attention to this passage.
15. Arnold Toynbee, *An Historian's Approach to Religion*, Oxford, 1956, Oxford University Press, (based on Toynbee's Gifford Lectures for 1952–53), p. 2.
16. ibid.
17. Arnold Toynbee, *Mankind and Mother Earth*, London, 1976, Oxford University Press, p. 3.
18. Stanley A. Cook, *The Study of Religions*, London, 1914, Adam & Charles Black, p. 26.
19. Miguel de Unamuno, *The Agony of Christianity and Essays on Faith*, London, 1974, Routledge & Kegan Paul, pp. 172–173. The quotation is taken from Unamuno's essay 'What is Truth?', which was first published in 1904. Translation by Anthony Kerrigan.
20. John Bowker, *The Sense of God*, p. 18.

21. ibid.
22. James W. Fowler, *Stages of Faith*, the Psychology of Human Development and the Quest for Meaning, San Francisco, 1980, Harper & Row, pp. 294–295.
23. James W. Fowler, Robin W. Lovin et. al., *Trajectories of Faith*, Five Life Stories, Nashville, 1980, Abingdon, p. 31.
24. ibid.
25. Harvey Cox, *Turning East*, pp. 80–81.
26. Northrop Frye, 'The Knowledge of Good and Evil', in Max Black (ed.), *The Morality of Scholarship*, New York, 1967, Cornell University Press, p. 4.
27. Joseph C. McClelland, 'Teacher of Religion: Professor or Guru?', *Studies in Religion/Sciences Religieuses*, Vol. 2 (1972), p. 232.
28. Robert A. McDermott, 'Religion as an Academic Discipline', *Cross Currents*, Vol. 18 (1968), p. 29.
29. ibid.
30. See Harvey Cox, *Turning East*, especially Chapter 4.
31. James W. Fowler, *Stages of Faith*, p. 132.
32. J. E. Marcia, 'Development and Validation of Ego Identity Status', *Journal of Personality and Social Psychology*, Vol. 3 (1966), pp. 551–558, quoted in Helen L. Bee and Sandra K. Mitchell, *The Developing Person*, New York, 1980, p. 611.

Chapter Seven

1. Michael Novak, *Ascent of the Mountain, Flight of the Dove*, An Invitation to Religious Studies, New York, 1978, (1971), Harper & Row, pp. 11–12.
2. M. F. C. Bourdillon and Meyer Fortes (eds.), *Sacrifice*, London, 1980, Academic Press, p. xviii note 2.
3. Aldous Huxley, *Those Barren Leaves*, Harmondsworth, 1967, (1925), Penguin, p. 288.
4. Winston L. King, *Introduction to Religion*, a Phenomenological Approach, New York, 1968, (this is a revised edition of King's *Introduction to Religion*, first published in 1954) Harper & Row, p. 22. My emphasis.
5. William Ernest Hocking, *The Meaning of God in Human Experience*, New Haven, 1928, (1912), Yale University Press, pp. 238–239.
6. Winston L. King, op. cit., p. 22.

7. Huston Smith, *The purposes of Higher Education*, p. 1.
8. R. S. Lee on p. 7 of his Introduction to Paul Pruyser's *Between Belief and Unbelief*, London, 1975, (1974), Sheldon Press.
9. James Haughton Woods, *The Value of Religious Facts*, p. 109.
10. M. K. Gandhi, *An Autobiography*, The Story of My Experiments with Truth, London, 1972, (1949), Cape, tr. Mahadev Desai, p. 60.
11. ibid., p. 102.
12. Mircea Eliade, *No Souvenirs*, p. 267.
13. R. C. Zaehner (ed.), *The Concise Encyclopedia of Living Faiths*, London, 1971, (1959), Hutchinson, p. xxi.
14. Stanley Samartha, 'The Lordship of Jesus Christ and Religious Pluralism', in Gerald H. Anderson and Thomas F. Stransky (eds.), *Christ's Lordship and Religious Pluralism*, p. 35.
15. Edward Hulmes, *Commitment and Neutrality in Religious Education*, London, 1979, Geoffrey Chapman, p. 103.
16. William Barrett, *Irrational Man*, A Study in Existential Philosophy, Connecticut, 1977, (1958), Greenwood Press, p. 5.
17. ibid., p. 6.
18. ibid., p. 5. Mircea Eliade, in terms very similar to Barrett's, draws our attention to the way in which specialization tends to obscure the sense of vocation which draws many to *the study of religions*: 'The present situation amounts to this: there has been a great advance in our knowledge of the material, which has been won at the cost of excessive specialization to the point of partly sacrificing our vocation.' ('Psychology and Comparative Religion: A Study of the Symbolism of the Centre', in Cecily Hastings and Donald Nicholl (eds.) *Selection II*, London, Sheed & Ward, 1954, p. 19).
19. R. G. Collingwood, *Speculum Mentis*, or the Map of Knowledge, Oxford, 1956, (1924), Oxford University Press, p. 15.
20. John Bowker, *The Sense of God*, p. 75.
21. Edwin Muir, 'The Child Dying', p. 67 in *Edwin Muir, Selected Poems*, ed. T. S. Eliot, London 1969, (1965), Faber.
22. R. W. Hepburn, *Christianity and Paradox*, London, 1966, (1953), Watts & Co., p. 200.
23. Rudolf Otto, *The Idea of the Holy*, pp. 72 and 155.
24. Ninian Smart, *Beyond Ideology*, p. 42.
25. David Hay, *Exploring Inner Space*, p. 198.
26. ibid.
27. Aldous Huxley, *Brave New World*, Harmondsworth, 1970, (1932), Penguin, p. 183.
28. See Hans Küng, *Does God Exist?*, London, 1980, (1978),

Collins, p. 607, and John Hick, 'Religious Pluralism', in Frank Whaling (ed.) *The World's Religious Traditions, Current Perspectives in Religious Studies*, Essays in Honour of Wilfred Cantwell Smith, Edinburgh, 1984, T & T Clark, p. 156.

29. The relevant passage from Haribhadra's *Story of Samaraditya* (2.55–80) is reprinted in translation in Wm. Theodore de Bary (ed.), *Sources of Indian Tradition*, Vol. 1 pp. 53–55; Tolstoy recounts this 'oriental fable' in Chapter 4 of his *My Confession*; William James cites Tolstoy in *The Varieties of Religious Experience*, when he deals in lectures 6 and 7 with the 'sick souled' outlook (pp. 159–161 in the 1974 Fontana paperback edition).

Name Index

Amiel, Henri-Frédéric, 27, 49, 87, 156n18
Austin, J. L., 105

Barbellion, 27
Baronté, Gervee, 39, 40
Barrett, William, 140, 141
Barth, Karl, 103
Bashkirtseff, Marie, 27
Becker, Ernest, 40
Beeblebrox, Zaphod, 12
Beethoven, 119
Berger, Peter, 8, 46, 76, 152n26
Beveridge, William, 13, 14
Black, Max, 12
Bleeker, C. J., 37, 41
Bourdillon, M. F. C., 131
Bowker, John, 106, 111, 120, 142
Britton, Karl, 11
Brown, Father, 82
Buddha, 7, 24, 25, 29, 43, 51, 54, 103, 106
Burhoe, Ralph Wendell, 36
Buridan, 147
Burnouf, Emile, 36

Cellini, Benvenuto, 60
Chardin, Teilhard de, 10
Chesterton, G. K., 82
Christian, William A., 110
Collingwood, R. G., 141, 156n18
Confucius, 8

Cook, Stanley A., 119
Cox, Harvey, 121, 125, 161n14
Cragg, A. K., 150n31
Cupitt, Don, 63

Dalai Lama, 12
Dalgleish, Adam, 10
Darwin, 36
D'Costa, Gavin, 150n31
Descartes, 31, 88
Dunne, John S., 79, 80, 156n18
Durkheim, Emile, 45

Eckhart, Meister, 101
Einstein, 26
Eliade, Mircea, 26, 27, 60, 84, 85, 138, 154n16, 163n18
Evans-Pritchard, E. E., 83

Farley, Edward, 98, 99
Finch, William, 33, 34
Flew, Antony, 77, 78
Fortes, Meyer, 131
Fowler, James, 121, 125
Freud, 45, 48
Frye, Northrop, 123, 124
Furriskey, John, 1, 2

Gandhi, 121, 137
Gaskin, J. C. A., 56, 63
Genghis Khan, 26
Ghazali, al-, 106
Gifford, Lord, ix, x
Gilgamesh, 25

Subject Index

Certain headings in the subject index are asterisked. This is to indicate their importance in the text and the impossibility of indexing them adequately. Several items have simply been omitted from the index for the same reason (*diversity*, *hall of mirrors*, *pluralism* etc.).